CULTURES OF THE WORLD
Costa Rica

Cavendish
Square

New York

Published in 2017 by Cavendish Square Publishing, LLC
243 5th Avenue, Suite 136, New York, NY 10016
Copyright © 2017 by Cavendish Square Publishing, LLC

Third Edition

This publication represents the opinions and views of the author based on his or her personal experience, knowledge, and research. The information in this book serves as a general guide only. The author and publisher have used their best efforts in preparing this book and disclaim liability rising directly or indirectly from the use and application of this book.
CPSIA Compliance Information: Batch #CS17CSQ
All websites were available and accurate when this book was sent to press.

Library of Congress Cataloging-in-Publication Data

Names: Foley, Erin, 1967- author. | Cooke, Barbara, 1966- author. | Ryckman, Tatiana, author.
Title: Costa Rica / Erin Foley, Barbara Cooke, and Tatiana Ryckman.
Description: New York : Cavendish Square Publishing, [2017] | Series: Cultures of the world | Includes bibliographical references and index.
Identifiers: LCCN 2016057411 (print) | LCCN 2016057662 (ebook) | ISBN 9781502626103 (library bound) | ISBN 9781502626035 (E-book)
Subjects: LCSH: Costa Rica--Juvenile literature.
Classification: LCC F1543.2 .F65 2017 (print) | LCC F1543.2 (ebook) | DDC 972.86--dc23
LC record available at https://lccn.loc.gov/2016057411

Editorial Director: David McNamara
Editor: Kristen Susienka
Copy Editor: Nathan Heidelberger
Associate Art Director: Amy Greenan
Designer: Alan Sliwinski
Production Coordinator: Karol Szymczuk
Photo Research: J8 Media

PICTURE CREDITS

Printed in the United States of America

CONTENTS

COSTA RICA TODAY

COSTA RICA STANDS OUT AMONG ITS CENTRAL AMERICAN neighbors for its extraordinary beauty and the warmth of its people. With a deep commitment to family ties, the environment, and democracy, Costa Rica is a paradise of natural beauty and enjoys relative peace, stability, and prosperity.

Home to one of the world's richest and most diverse natural environments, Costa Rica has also set an outstanding example in its approach to conservation. Regularly lauded as one of the most eco-friendly countries on Earth, Costa Rica relies on renewable energy for power and has developed an impressive system of national parks and wildlife refuges. Even as the government works to actively protect the environment, it faces pressure to remove protections on wildlife and forested land from fishermen and farmers concerned about their livelihoods.

NATIVE COMMUNITIES

Like many of its neighboring countries, Costa Rica was first colonized by Spanish explorers in the 1500s and has integrated Spanish traditions with its native

Farming has long been an integral part of the Costa Rican identity.

culture. As a result, Spanish is the national language, Roman Catholicism the national religion, and even the arts are inspired by classical European styles. While the native population originally suffered from exposure to new diseases brought from Europe, from being enslaved, or just from being forced into a new way of life, today greater effort is being made to protect indigenous populations and their lifestyle. Natives and their lands are protected by the government, and a few schools have even opened to teach the native languages of various tribes in Costa Rica to keep them alive.

For its relatively homogenous population of mostly Spanish descent, life is a balance of tradition and progress. Costa Ricans, who refer to themselves as *ticos* (TEE-kohs), strive to get on in life through hard work and education, yet they continue to respect conservative values, especially when it comes to family matters. A country that remains true to its ideals, it is one of the oldest democracies in the region and one of the few countries in the world that has abolished its military, preferring instead to invest in education for its people. This strong focus on education has resulted in a 98 percent literacy rate, significantly higher than neighboring Nicaragua (83 percent) and even slightly higher than international hub Panama (95 percent).

FARMING ROOTS AND NEW TECHNOLOGIES

Costa Rica's national identity is that of the yeoman farmer, an independent farmer who works his own plot of land with his family. For decades, Costa Ricans developed a strong agricultural base for their economy, exporting coffee and bananas. Recently, however, the country has been developing its manufacturing sector and has begun exporting medical equipment and circuit boards. Another source of national income is the tourism industry, which brought a record-breaking 2.6 million visitors to the country in 2015.

STRUGGLES FACED

While Costa Rica has seen huge gains in prosperity and education in the past thirty years, these have been accompanied by growing pains. As industry improves and machination takes over, the ideal of the independent yeoman farmer becomes less plausible. Important environmental protections also limit the land that can be cleared to raise cattle or farm, or prohibit certain species of fish from being caught. This has resulted in a widening wage gap, leaving a greater portion of the population struggling financially while a smaller group of professionals enjoys a larger portion of the improved economy. Housing, for instance, has become hard to secure as housing prices in the most populous parts of the country become out of reach even for middle-class families.

The Costa Rican government is sensitive to this dynamic and is constantly negotiating the country's many interests—the environment, economic well-being, and education. The government is run in accordance with the 1949 constitution, which was drafted on the heels of Costa Rica's civil war. The constitution was remarkable for both abolishing the military—a source of great pride for Costa Ricans—and for declaring that a healthy, natural environment is a human right.

Despite the natural growing pains Costa Rica faces as it integrates itself on the world stage, it remains a shining example of personal liberties, peace, and ecological policy. The people, like their surroundings, are known for their warmth and hospitality.

GEOGRAPHY

Costa Rica is known for its fertile soil, rich biodiversity, and varied geography.

1

L ITERALLY TRANSLATING TO "RICH coast," Costa Rica is full of exotic animals, agricultural land for fruits and coffee, and beaches. Costa Rica's diverse geographical regions are to thank for the nation's natural beauty and abundance.

GEOGRAPHICAL REGIONS

Costa Rica's rich natural biodiversity covers the small country's varied geography, which can be divided into three main regions: the Pacific coastal area, the central highlands, and the Caribbean lowlands. The narrow Pacific coastal region rises steeply into the central highlands, which then descend more gradually into the Caribbean plain on the eastern side of the nation.

PACIFIC COAST The Pacific lowlands are characterized by steep cliffs and narrow white-sand beaches. The northern portion of the Pacific coast is known as the Gold Coast because it is consistently dry, warm, and sunny. This area, bordering Nicaragua, receives the least rainfall of any part of the country.

The Pacific coastline broadens into three peninsulas. The northernmost peninsula, the Nicoya Peninsula, juts to the southeast to form the Gulf of Nicoya. The southern Costa Rican peninsula, Osa, forms the Gulf of Dulce. The southern boundary runs through a narrow third peninsula, which terminates in Punta Burica. An alluvial (matter

• • • • • • • • • • • •

The Cordillera de Talamanca includes the Chirripó Grande, the highest point in Costa Rica at 12,530 feet (3,819 m).

The southern portion of the Pacific coast is home to lush rain forests and is sparsely inhabited, preserving its pristine natural beauty.

deposited by running water) coastal plain runs from the Osa Peninsula to the port of Puntarenas on the Gulf of Nicoya. This southern portion of the Pacific coast is home to humid rain forests and has a low population density. Steep coastal mountain cliffs break the otherwise monotonous landscape of the coastal plains, whose northern end widens into the Valle de Tempisque.

CENTRAL HIGHLANDS The Central Valley is formed at the point where the southeastern end of the Cordillera Central runs parallel to the northwestern point of the Cordillera de Talamanca. The major portion of the Central Valley consists of two smaller basins making up the populous Meseta Central. Almost two-thirds of the population of Costa Rica inhabits this temperate area of about 3,900 square miles (10,100 square kilometers).

Influenced by the Caribbean climate, the Cartago basin to the east has heavier rainfall and higher humidity, in spite of its higher elevation of about 4,930 feet (1,503 meters) above sea level. The San José basin lies northwest of Cartago. Costa Rica's capital city, San José, and its sprawling suburbs are located here. With a more temperate climate and elevation of approximately 3,773 feet (1,150 m), the San José basin produces much of Costa Rica's cash crop, coffee. Another large basin, the General Valley, lies to the south. Until the 1940s, this area was relatively isolated. The construction of the Pan-American Highway after World War II, however, opened up the area to farmers.

Many tropical cloud forests are found at higher elevations, from approximately 3,300 feet to 9,800 feet (1,000 m to 3,000 m). In these very high environments, clouds continually drench the forest with a fine mist, nourishing a variety of plants. The Monteverde Cloud Forest Reserve in Costa Rica, the largest cloud forest in Central America, has been preserved as a national park. The *páramo* (PAH-rah-moh), a special, treeless environment with sparse, hardy grasses spreads across the highest elevations, above 9,800 feet (3,000 m).

CARIBBEAN LOWLANDS Costa Rica's Caribbean coast is made up of lowlands that extend into much of the northern and inland areas of the country. This region has a diverse population of natives, Caribbean immigrants, and expats. It is a geographical continuation of the broad lowlands of Nicaragua and has an average elevation of less than 400 feet (120 m) above sea level. The Caribbean coast is lined with numerous white- and black-sand (from crushed lava flow) beaches, while the Caribbean lowlands constitute nearly one-fifth of Costa Rica's total land area. The region consists mainly of flat plains irrigated by streams flowing from the central highlands. The lowlands in the north also have a scattering of hills and volcanoes.

Because of their high elevation, cloud forests are watered by the mist of passing clouds.

GEOGRAPHY AND CLIMATE

The Republic of Costa Rica, with an area of 19,730 square miles (51,100 sq km), is the third-smallest country in Central America, after El Salvador and Belize. It is slightly smaller than the state of West Virginia. Costa Rica lies between 8° and 11° north of the equator, extending from the northwest to the southeast along the lower portion of the Central American isthmus.

It is bordered by the countries of Nicaragua to the north and Panama to the south and southeast, and by the Caribbean Sea to the northeast and the Pacific Ocean to the west and southwest. Its Caribbean coast is only

Covering 200 square miles (518 sq km), the Irazú volcano is highly active, erupting about every twenty years or less. Researchers have discovered that during a dramatic explosion in 1963, magma rushed up from deep within Earth to its surface in just a few months—significantly faster than the thousands of years they used to believe it took for magma to reach Earth's crust. They call the pathway that leads from Earth's mantle to its crust a "highway from hell" for its quick delivery of fiery magma.

The 1963 eruption of Irazú took place while the US president, John F. Kennedy, was visiting Costa Rica. But the eruption lasted much longer than the president's visit—it continued for two years, blanketing the capital city of San José with 5 inches (13 centimeters) of muddy ash that killed twenty people, destroyed crops, and killed cattle.

Although it was an immediate disaster for the economy and the people living in San José, the huge deposit of volcanic ash enriched the soil of the Meseta Central (Central Valley) for decades thereafter. This area produces much of Costa Rica's food, and the produce the country exports, ultimately helping the economy.

Irazú last erupted in 1994, but this more recent activity caused little damage.

185 miles (300 km) long, while its Pacific coastline stretches nearly 630 miles (1,015 km). At its broadest point, the country extends to approximately 174 miles (280 km) from coast to coast, while narrowing to less than 75 miles (120 km) across at its narrowest point.

TOPOGRAPHY AND GEOLOGY Two major mountain chains, running from the northwest to southeast, constitute the interior highlands of Costa Rica: the Cordillera Volcánica, which starts in the northwest, and the Cordillera de Talamanca in the south. The word *cordillera* means "mountain range." As suggested by its name, the Cordillera Volcánica includes several volcanoes. The Cordillera Volcánica actually consists of three continuous mountain ranges: the northwestern Cordillera de Guanacaste, the smaller Cordillera Tilarán, and the Cordillera Central. The de Guanacaste and the Central chains both include several volcanic peaks. Two of the volcanoes in the Cordillera Central—Poás at 8,870 feet (2,704 m) and Irazú at 11,257 feet (3,431 m)—are still active.

Near the middle of the country, the northern point of the Cordillera de Talamanca begins parallel to the southernmost point of the Cordillera Central. Their highland elevations merge to form the Central Valley, which historically has attracted the greatest number of inhabitants.

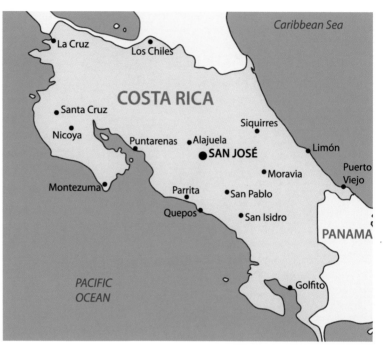

Most of Costa Rica's population lives on the fertile plateau in the middle of the country, around the capital city, San José.

EARTHQUAKES   It is not unusual to feel tremors regularly in Costa Rica. During a two-month period in 1989, seismologists recorded more than sixteen thousand tremors, although only sixteen of them registered above 4.0 on the Richter scale.

Costa Rica is located along a geological fault system where the Pacific Ocean's Cocos plate meets the tectonic plate underlying the Caribbean. The country is therefore subject to occasional and sometimes devastating earthquakes.

Several earthquakes have affected Costa Rica in varying degrees. An earthquake on January 8, 2009, killed thirty-four people around the village of Cinchona. Only a few years before, on November 20, 2004, an earthquake was felt just outside San José. It was not quite as strong as the one that hit the Caribbean town of Pandora in 1991. That quake, measuring 7.4 on the Richter scale, was the strongest earthquake felt in Costa Rica since a 1910 quake that killed 1,750 people. The 1991 quake caused only superficial

Costa Rica regularly experiences earthquakes, which can cause devastating loss of life and damages.

structural damage in San José, 70 miles (113 km) away from Pandora, but it wreaked devastation on the Caribbean coastal areas. Twenty-seven people were reported killed, but more than four hundred people were injured and thirteen thousand left homeless.

The 1991 earthquake permanently changed Costa Rica's landscape. The port city of Puerto Limón, for instance, rose in elevation by almost 5 feet (1.5 m), as did other parts of the coastline. As a result, some canals are now too high to connect with the Atlantic Ocean. The quake also raised coral reefs in some places, killing the coral exposed to air, and leaving only their skeletal remains jutting out of the water.

In 2012, a 7.6-magnitude earthquake hit the Nicoya Peninsula on the Pacific coast. While the quake was vigorous, causing structural damage to buildings and electrical outages, there was relatively little loss of human life. One resident died of a heart attack, and a construction worker died when a wall collapsed on him.

RIVERS Costa Rica is well irrigated by many rivers and streams. Most of the rivers have sources in the central highlands and flow into either the Caribbean Sea or the Pacific Ocean. The principal Pacific-flowing rivers include the Río Grande de Tárcoles and the Río Grande de Térraba, which is fed by tributaries rising out of the General Valley. The main rivers flowing to the Caribbean Sea include the Reventazón and the San Juan. The San Juan River originates from Lake Nicaragua, within Nicaragua, and forms a major part of the international boundary with that country.

In an effort to reduce their use of nonrenewable energy, Costa Ricans have harnessed hydropower from their many rivers.

Rivers in Costa Rica are used for practical purposes, such as watering crops, being converted for hydroelectric power, or providing the main source of transportation through isolated areas by riverboat and canoe. But the rivers also provide excellent nature-observing opportunities, supporting the economy through tourism and providing a habitat for the region's robust wildlife.

CLIMATE AND SEASONS Given its proximity to the equator, Costa Rica is a tropical country. Its climate, however, varies according to elevation and, to a lesser degree, to the amount of annual rainfall in different locations. The average temperature on the coast varies from about 77°F to 93°F (25°C to 34°C), while the average temperature in the highlands is 72°F (22°C).

There are two definite seasons: *verano* (beh-RAH-noh) and *invierno* (een-bee-AIR-noh). These terms are translated as "summer" and "winter," respectively. In Costa Rica, verano refers specifically to the dry season and invierno to the rainy season.

Costa Rica experiences summer, or the dry season, at the end of the year, during North America's winter. Usually beginning around mid-November, verano signals the coffee harvest and Christmas season. The wet season, on the other hand, occurs in the middle of the year. The rainy season generally lasts from April or May through October or November, with the heaviest rainfall in September and October. During the rainy season, several days may pass with no interruption in the downpour.

ENVIRONMENT AND WILDLIFE

Costa Rica has twelve distinct ecological zones, with a diverse range of plant and animal life. Because of its tropical location and variety of ecological zones, including both tropical rain forests and tropical dry forests, Costa Rica is bursting with botanical variety. About 20 percent of the country is covered with forests of broadleaf evergreen trees, such as oak, mahogany, and tropical cedar trees. There are over 2,000 distinct species of trees and 9,000 kinds of flowering plants, including more than 1,200 species of Costa Rica's national flower, the orchid.

FLORA The tropical dry forests do not receive rain during verano and are vulnerable to accidental fires. As the drought ends in April, the leafy trees—

Costa Rica's national flower, the orchid, grows abundantly in the country's humid climate.

including the purple jacaranda, pink and white meadow oak, and bright-orange flame-of-the-forest—explode into bursts of colors. Because of the lack of moisture for six months of the year, tropical dry forests are not as densely forested as tropical rain forests. These arid zones have only two basic layers: the treetops and ground-level bushes.

While the dry forests have sparse vegetation and only two layers, tropical rain forests are densely packed with several layers of plant and animal life. Each layer, from the treetop canopy to the ground floor of the forest, provides a suitable habitat for different forms of life. Humidity is high due to year-round rain, long hours of sunlight, and high temperatures. This mix of environmental factors creates ideal conditions for the proliferation of innumerable types of fungi, molds, ferns, vines, trees, and bushes.

COASTAL VEGETATION The coastal areas are characterized by palm trees or, in certain areas, by mangroves, which are trees uniquely adapted to surviving in salty coastal habitats. Mangroves choke portions of the shoreline, especially along the Nicoya and Dulce Gulfs, with their interlocking, stilt-like roots. Costa Rica is home to five different species of the mangrove. Their shallow roots draw nutrients from the surface of their swampy surroundings, while patches of spongy tissue on their bark enable them to absorb oxygen from the air. While palm trees are prolific along the Caribbean coast, they have also been transplanted to the Pacific lowlands, where plantations of African palms have been established.

FAUNA The country's many ecological zones also foster an astounding variety of animal, insect, and bird life, which can be attributed to Costa Rica's unique location as a bridge between North and South America.

Costa Rica has an estimated 160 species of amphibians and more than 200 species of reptiles, over half of which are snakes, including some venomous vipers like the fer-de-lance and bushmaster. Most of the amphibian species are frogs and toads, many of which are brightly colored. The most commonly spotted reptile is the green iguana, which can grow to more than 6 feet (1.8 m) long. Both land-dwelling and aquatic turtles found in the Caribbean

Some orchids are so minuscule that they measure less than 0.04 inches (1 millimeter) in diameter. Others have hanging petals that are more than 1.5 feet (46 cm) long. The majority of orchids are epiphytes, taking root on trees or other plants, although in a nonparasitic fashion.

In 2015, a new species of frog was discovered. The Kermit look-alike is called Diane's bare-hearted glass frog for its translucent skin and visible internal organs.

lowlands were once common but are now critically endangered. Crocodiles and their smaller relatives, caimans, inhabit the wet lowlands of both coasts.

Costa Rica is home to about 200 species of mammals, half of which are bats. Many species have been hunted to extinction, while others remain endangered. Habitat destruction due to deforestation poses the greatest threat to the jaguar, the largest and most powerful member of the American cat family. The tapir, a stout, pig-like animal, is also under fire due to overhunting. Most of those remaining are now only found in areas where hunting is restricted, further establishing the importance of protected wildlife areas.

In addition to mammals and amphibians, more than 850 species of birds have been identified in Costa Rica. The endangered resplendent quetzal—a sacred bird for the ancient Mayas and Aztecs, who once lived in Central America—and scarlet macaw are considered the "rare jewels" of the country; fortunately, both are plentiful in the protected reserves. Other colorful birds include the laughing falcon, tanager, blue-footed booby, and six different species of the toucan.

Although several thousand known species of insects inhabit Costa Rica, many more remain unidentified. The blue morpho butterfly and leaf-cutter ants are just some of the insects that can be found. The country has thousands of species of ants, and more species of butterflies than all of Africa. On a single tree in the rain forest, entomologists (scientists who study insects) have collected over 950 species of beetles.

HUMAN HABITATS

Costa Rica has six major urban areas: San José, Cartago, Heredia, and Alajuela, which constitute the four colonial cities of the Central Valley; Puntarenas

on the Pacific coast; and Puerto Limón on the Caribbean Sea. Roughly two-thirds of the country's population of 4.8 million lives in the Central Valley.

SAN JOSÉ The capital city dominates national life in Costa Rica. It is the political, cultural, and economic center of the country. In the early 1940s, its population was only seventy thousand, and villages and coffee groves surrounded the city. After World War II, many people migrated from the rural areas to the capital in search of better-paying jobs. The city sprawled outward in all directions, incorporating surrounding villages and coffee fields into the suburbs of San José. Unfortunately, this urban sprawl occurred with no planning or zoning. The basic infrastructure lagged behind the new growth, and even today, streets, water supply, and sewage disposal are often inadequate or nonexistent. However, suburbs, especially those around San Pedro, are tranquil and have a steady supply of potable, safe-to-drink water.

San José is the cultural center of Costa Rica, but it is also home to many impoverished citizens who live in slums or shantytowns.

In sharp contrast, low- and middle-income neighborhoods, shantytowns, and fashionable neighborhoods are often erected side by side. In the midst of the modern concrete architecture of San José, historic structures, such as the National Theater, remain. Most were built in the latter part of the nineteenth century or the early part of the twentieth century. Most colonial-era architecture has not survived the major earthquakes.

Josefinos (ho-say FEE-nohs), as San José residents are known, number about 288,000. Including outlying areas, the population reaches about 2.1 million. The downtown area is congested with cars, and pedestrians spill onto the streets because the sidewalks are often cracked and broken or packed with vendors. The air is filled with diesel and gas fumes, and the constant din of motor vehicles, shouting vendors, and ongoing construction can be overwhelming. In spite of its urban congestion, San José still attracts tourists and residents with its vibrant nightlife, national symphony orchestra, museums, art galleries, restaurants, and an international flavor.

PUNTARENAS AND PUERTO LIMÓN Puntarenas is a city of about seventy thousand people, situated on the Gulf of Nicoya. It was the principal port on the Pacific coast until a deepwater port, Puerto Caldera, was constructed about 10 miles (16 km) to the south. Today, fishing constitutes the primary occupation and industry of Puntarenas.

Puerto Limón achieved prominence during the latter half of the nineteenth century as an export center for coffee and bananas being shipped to European markets. The city of Limón is Costa Rica's principal port city and is its most important city on the Caribbean coast, though the population has steadily declined in recent years. The population has fallen from 94,400 in 2011 to around 58,500 in 2016. Regrettably, it is one of the poorest and most neglected areas of the country.

INTERNET LINKS

http://travel.nationalgeographic.com/travel/countries/costa-rica-guide
National Geographic has maps and travel information about countries all over the world, including Costa Rica.

http://www.worldatlas.com/webimage/countrys/namerica/camerica/cr.htm
The World Atlas website features geographical information about Costa Rica.

HISTORY

Many Costa Ricans still wear traditional garb when celebrating historical and cultural events.

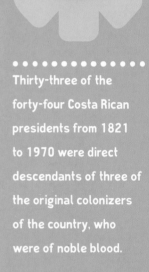

2

A RCHAEOLOGISTS HAVE FOUND evidence of civilizations in Costa Rica as far back as ten thousand years ago. These indigenous, or native, groups often fought with each other, but they gradually developed advanced tools, artworks, and weaponry.

Thirty-three of the forty-four Costa Rican presidents from 1821 to 1970 were direct descendants of three of the original colonizers of the country, who were of noble blood.

When Europeans arrived in the early 1500s, they found five main indigenous groups dwelling there. As is the case throughout the Americas, the conflict between natives and settlers was contentious and often violent. The history of Costa Rica as a unified and independent nation, however, starts with these Spanish settlers, and progresses to its relatively prosperous present-day status. Settlers worked their own plots of land, and gradually a poor but proud and self-reliant society emerged. Thus, the image of the yeoman farmer is imprinted on Costa Rica's national consciousness.

DISCOVERING COSTA RICA

Historically, the territory of present-day Costa Rica was sparsely populated in comparison with other areas of Central America. At the time of the Spanish conquest in the sixteenth century, more than twenty-five thousand natives lived in the area. They were broadly divided into five groups: the Chorotega, Carib, Boruca, Corobicí, and Nahua. Rather than uniting, they constantly fought for control of the territory. When victorious, they exacted tribute from their vanquished

Pre-Columbian artifacts like this tripod vase give historians clues about the lives and values of ancient cultures.

enemies in the form of gold and prisoners, whom they used as slaves or as offerings in ritual sacrifice. Many of their religious ceremonies and crafts reflected Mayan influence.

These early civilizations used beans as currency and spun cotton into threads for weaving cloth. They were also skilled metalworkers, crafting ornaments and other objects from gold that they imported from other regions. The indigenous inhabitants fiercely resisted the Spanish invasion, and some fled into the rain forest, where they continued to resist Spanish rule long after colonization.

SPANISH CONQUEST

Christopher Columbus was the first European to set foot on the coast of what is now Costa Rica. On his fourth voyage to the Americas, on September 18, 1502, he landed at Cariay, the site of today's Caribbean Puerto Limón. Columbus established relations with the indigenous groups, who greeted him with gifts of gold. Spanish adventurers were later drawn to the area in their search for gold. Successive explorers began to think of this area as "the rich coast," and thus called it Costa Rica. The larger area—present-day Costa Rica, Panama, and yet unexplored parts of the isthmus—was called Veragua.

The Spanish colonized much of what is now Central America, forming several provinces. However, they found the indigenous groups of Costa Rica difficult to subdue. The impenetrable jungle and new diseases that were native to Costa Rica further impeded their conquest. Their efforts were not helped by their constant infighting, as different groups competed with each other to find gold. In 1539, the area of Costa Rica was separated from Veragua and officially named Costa Rica.

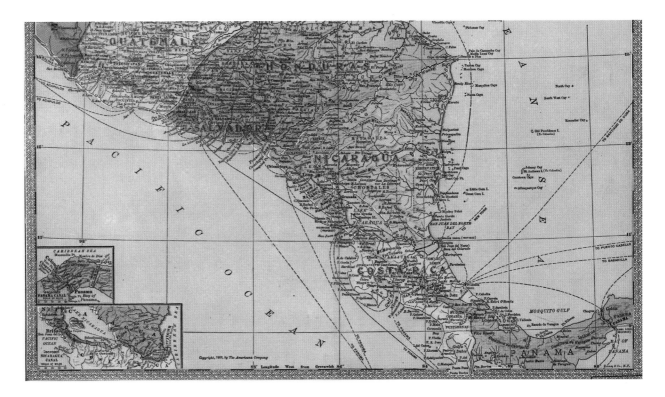

It was not until 1561 that Juan de Cavallón, governor of Costa Rica, succeeded in colonizing the Caribbean coast. He established the settlement of Garcimuñoz in 1561, but he left in 1562, discouraged by the lack of gold. Juan Vásquez de Coronado replaced him as governor, and in 1564 he relocated the base settlement to the fertile highlands and named it Cartago. The new settlement provided an agricultural base to sustain further exploration and colonization of the territory.

EARLY ELITE

Costa Rican society during the colonial period was made up of two basic social classes. The *hidalgos*, or gentry of Costa Rican society, formed the ruling class and were called by the honorary titles of *don*, or "sir," or *doña*, or "madam." The commoners were collectively known as *plebeyos* (play-BAY-yohs), literally translated as "plebeians," or commoners. The settlers—both hidalgos and plebeyos—worked their own lands, which made it difficult for

Veragua was the original name for the territory spanning the narrow land bridge. It wasn't until Spanish settlers came in search of gold that the land was divided into countries, including Costa Rica.

Hidalgos were not necessarily wealthy. Often these modest farmers were accepted in higher social circles based on their family name and ancestry.

anyone to amass large holdings. In this aspect, Costa Rica was unique among its Central American neighbors.

The hidalgos were not wealthy compared with the gentry of other Central American societies. More often than not, they were the sons of poor Spanish families who came to America to seek their fortunes. In Costa Rica, they ended up as farmers who enjoyed certain privileges because of their family name. For instance, only the hidalgos were allowed to serve on the municipal councils, and they received a deference from the plebeyos.

Thus, Costa Rica started out as a very poor colony without great economic opportunities for its settlers. On the other hand, the poverty of its landholders, combined with the lack of a large underclass, gave rise to a more equitable class structure than any that existed in Spain and in most of the other Spanish colonies.

COLONIAL PERIOD

In 1573, the Spanish crown fixed permanent boundaries for Costa Rica, which still had only two settlements, Cartago and Aranjuez. The territory, physically isolated from the rest of Central America, stagnated as one of the most backward and neglected possessions of Spain's American empire. During the Spanish conquest, the Native Americans were driven out of their traditional territories, and many were killed as a result of ongoing warfare between indigenous groups, attacks from the Spanish invaders, rampant new diseases introduced by the Spanish, and starvation.

Many of the surviving tribes became Christians, especially the Chorotegas. As Christians, they were allowed to remain in their own villages under their traditional leaders if they wished, or they could move into the Hispanic settlements, where they intermarried and were quickly assimilated into the mestizo (mixed-blood) population. The only remaining purely Native American population isolated itself in the Talamanca region.

Within a few generations after the conquest, the Costa Rican population had assumed a generally mestizo character that identified completely with Spanish culture. The small number of black slaves that the Spanish originally brought to the territory integrated into the Hispanic community along with most of the indigenous groups. As was the case in other parts of Latin America, the Spanish settlers forced the native people into servitude during the late sixteenth and early seventeenth centuries. This system failed in the long run in Costa Rica, however, because the local population was too small to exploit as a labor force. The settler population also grew more slowly than in other regions, as the country yielded no mineral or other native resources and was relatively unattractive to most immigrants.

Though slavery was practiced in Costa Rica, the native population and imported African slaves were too few, and the practice eventually failed.

A MOVE FOR INDEPENDENCE

By the early 1800s, the Spanish Empire had been weakened due to Napoleon Bonaparte's conquest of Spain, and they gradually lost their South and Central American influence. First, in August 1821, Mexico declared independence. At the time, Costa Rica was governed by proxy by Guatemala, which had been the Spanish administrative center, as part of the Capitanía General de Guatemala. Thus, when Guatemala unilaterally declared the independence of all the Central American provinces, Costa Rica gained independence as well.

Because a large portion of the ruling class was of Spanish descent, Costa Ricans were initially unsure whether they should remain loyal to the crown or move forward with independence. The municipal councils of the four principal towns of Heredia, Cartago, Alajuela, and San José met separately to try to decide.

Simón Bolívar is an icon for many Costa Ricans.

While the Costa Ricans were waiting to decide their future, the newly proclaimed "emperor" of Mexico, Augustín I, demanded that the Central American provinces submit to his authority. Again, the principal Costa Rican towns were divided in their response. Heredia and Cartago voted to unite with an imperialist Mexico, while Alajuela and San José rejected Mexico in favor of either uniting with another Central American province or becoming an independent republic. This conflict sparked a civil war between the towns in December 1822. After a one-day battle, the republican forces from Alajuela and San José defeated the imperialist troops from Heredia and Cartago.

SIMÓN BOLÍVAR

Independence hero Simón Bolívar hoped for the unification of Latin America. In March 1823, Costa Rica finally declared its independence from Spain, and five months later, it joined with the United Provinces of Central America, also known as the Central American Federation. However, competing interests and civil war prevented its effectiveness. The Central American Federation was doomed to collapse, as it was torn by war and strife. Like many of the nations in the federation, Costa Rica withdrew and reentered its membership, first leaving in 1829 and rejoining the union nine months later. The entire federation disintegrated within a decade and was officially disbanded in February 1839.

Although the federation existed for only sixteen years, it stood as a symbol of regional unification that many Central Americans still desire.

A YOUNG NATION

In contrast to the tumultuous history of most of its neighbors, Costa Ricans have generally managed to avoid violent political and social upheavals. Even so, during the 1830s, Costa Rica was again torn by conflict as the principal towns competed to be the capital.

In 1834, the newly elected head of state, Braulio Carrillo Colina, established San José as the capital, which provoked a rebellion by the other three towns. In 1838, Carrillo lost his bid for reelection; however, he immediately seized control of the government as a dictator. Three years later, he abolished the constitution and declared himself dictator for life.

During his four-year dictatorship, he took steps to advance the political and economic interests of Costa Rica. In addition to reorganizing the government and establishing a new legal code, he encouraged the development of the coffee industry, at the same time encouraging an increase in the number of small landholders. In 1842, Carrillo was overthrown by his opponents, and a few years of instability followed.

In 1847, the congress appointed José María Castro Madriz as the first official president. In 1848, he formally declared Costa Rica an independent republic and approved a reform constitution, leading to his reputation as the "Founder of the Republic." The new constitution, like those before it, was inspired by the European Enlightenment. It confirmed the right to freedom of expression and association, and emphasized the importance of education. Suffrage, or the right to vote, however, was limited to men who were literate and owned property.

In 1849, Castro Madriz was forced to resign by a coalition of coffee barons and disgruntled army officers who opposed his reform policies and his inability to quell rising unrest. He was succeeded by Juan Rafael Mora Porras, a coffee planter and member of an important political family.

José María Castro was the first official president of Costa Rica, elected in 1847.

ECONOMIC PROGRESS AND SETBACKS FOR DEMOCRACY Although the glory of victory shone on President Mora Porras for a brief time, having defeated American William Walker's troops in 1857, the high cost of that victory ultimately led to his overthrow. More than a decade later, in 1870, the presidency was again overthrown, this time by General Tomás Guardia Gutiérrez, who quickly assumed dictatorial powers and ruled until his death in 1882.

In 1855 a political faction in neighboring Nicaragua hired William Walker, an American adventurer from Tennessee, to overthrow Nicaragua's president. After deposing the incumbent, however, Walker seized the presidency for himself and reintroduced slavery in Nicaragua.

Outraged by this infringement of national sovereignty, Costa Rican president Mora Porras declared war on Walker and his regime in February 1856. Mora Porras was able to raise an army of nine thousand men, which Walker confronted with several hundred of his mercenaries, or private soldiers. The Costa Ricans attacked Walker's forces in the town of Rivas, across the Nicaraguan border. A drummer boy by the name of Juan Santamaría succeeded in setting fire to Walker's stronghold, driving his men out from their cover. Santamaría lost his life in the ensuing action but is remembered as a national hero in Costa Rica.

Other Central American troops soon joined Costa Rica and defeated Walker in April 1857. The war against Walker, nevertheless, was very costly to Costa Rica. Almost half the Costa Rican troops died, either in battle or from diseases resulting from poor conditions in the military camps. Even with its enormous losses, the war became an event of great national pride and importance. While Costa Rica had previously been split by regional interests, the war united the country and inspired a sense of national unity.

While he restricted civil liberties, Guardia Gutiérrez tried to redistribute land and wealth. He also modernized the country, improving public schools, sanitation and public works, and the transportation network. He incurred a large national debt, however, which took the country several decades to repay.

Guardia Gutiérrez's greatest contribution to Costa Rica may have been the railroad project that he initiated in 1871. He hired an American, Minor Cooper Keith, to build a railroad from the Meseta Central to the Caribbean coast, connecting the cities of Alajuela and Puerto Limón. Immigrant labor, mostly from Italy, China, and Jamaica, helped to complete the twenty-year project. Some four thousand lives were lost from injuries and disease in the construction project, which cost about $8 million, but the railroad contributed greatly to Costa Rica's economic development. It attracted foreign entrepreneurs and opened up the Pacific coast, while also encouraging the growth of the banana industry.

The banana industry was dominated by foreign companies, owned primarily by North American businessmen. This meant that the profits generated from the export of bananas were not kept within Costa Rica. A major banana export company was Minor Keith's United Fruit Company, established in 1899. It controlled large areas of land and was very involved in Costa Rican politics. It also provided the impetus for the practice of legal racial segregation in Costa Rica between Hispanic workers and workers of African descent.

Over the next few decades Costa Rica became more democratic. Voting rights were expanded, but elections in the 1920s and 1930s were built upon a system of personalized political patronage, and rival liberals ruled the presidency for twelve years. The liberal philosophy opposed taxation on personal wealth and desired a limited role for a government freed from influence by the Catholic Church and widespread opportunities for education.

Ferrocarril Al Pacifico — Puente Rio Grande Costa Rica.

Though expensive in both money and lives, the railroad connecting Costa Rica's two coasts brought economic development to the small country.

CIVIL WAR AND REVOLUTION

By the 1930s, Costa Rica's long emphasis on the benefits of education produced a more politically astute citizenry and a relatively large middle class. This increased political awareness, however, prompted people to join various interest groups. City workers, farmers, and the urban middle class organized strikes as well as demonstrations in attempts to influence national policies. Suffrage for women and illiterates alike was introduced, and citizenship was conferred on all who were born in Costa Rica, meaning that Afro-Caribbeans born there were finally included among the citizens of Costa Rica.

Rafael Ángel Calderón Guardia was elected in 1940 through the powerful backing of the National Republican Party, which represented politicians and bureaucrats. His administration was marked by genuine social and economic reforms, such as reconciliation between church and state and an attempt to amend the constitution to allow a greater role for the government in certain issues. Many liberals, however, became outraged by Calderón's promulgation of the Social Guarantee amendments and by his expropriation of immigrant-owned properties during World War II. The Social Guarantees were a set of fifteen constitutional amendments that allowed congress to legislate such measures as a labor code, social security, health insurance, and the right of squatters to obtain titles to uncommitted land that they had cultivated.

Banana plantations in Central America were both lucrative for their foreign owners and economically and environmentally devastating to their homeland.

Meanwhile, the beginning of the twentieth century marked a period of ongoing conflicts with Costa Rica's neighbors, Nicaragua and Panama. In 1916, Costa Rica protested an agreement between Nicaragua and the United States. The agreement gave the United States the perpetual right to build a canal across the isthmus through Nicaraguan territory, using Costa Rica's portion of the San Juan River. Although the Central American Court of Justice sided with Costa Rica, the United States and Nicaragua ignored the judgment—thereby discrediting the court and ultimately causing its dissolution.

Costa Rica also had a long-standing border dispute with Panama concerning the definition of the boundary through the Sixaola basin on the Caribbean coast. In 1900, the French president arbitrated the dispute and awarded the area to Panama. Costa Rica protested. In 1914 the chief justice of the US Supreme Court arbitrated and awarded the area to Costa Rica—raising a protest from Panama. In 1921, the dispute escalated into armed hostilities when Costa Rica attempted to expel Panamanian residents in the Coto region on the Pacific coast. The United States intervened and evacuated the Panamanians. Relations between Costa Rica and Panama were broken off until an agreement was reached in 1941, ceding much of the disputed area to Costa Rica.

Amid rising political and civil unrest, the 1948 election was the most divisive the country had ever experienced. Otilio Ulate Blanco represented the National Union Party and was supported by the newly established Social Democratic Party. Ulate won by ten thousand votes against Calderón, who was seeking reelection through the National Republican Party. Each side accused the other of fraud, forcing the Election Commission to examine the issue. While two members of the commission upheld Ulate's victory, the third member disagreed, so the sitting president demanded that the legislature decide the election. The congress, which was filled with Calderón supporters, annulled the election altogether and appointed Calderón as president.

Ulate refused to concede defeat, and an armed force of volunteers was quickly assembled on his behalf. The head of this army, José Figueres Ferrer, was a landowner who had been exiled for two years for publicly opposing Calderón's policies in 1942. He gathered roughly six hundred men, mostly

Rural government troops prepared to enter a civil war after the contentious appointment of Rafael Ángel Calderón Guardia.

students and the sons of farmers, to form the National Liberation Army. On March 12, 1948, the civil war began, but the government was ill prepared to defend itself. The revolutionaries won the month-long war, calling it the War of National Liberation. A pact was signed by the two sides on April 19, 1948.

The civil war was the bloodiest period for native Costa Ricans. About two thousand people lost their lives, with many more wounded during the battle.

Acting as a temporary president, José Figueres extended the right to vote to women and established a modern democracy.

THE MODERN PERIOD

After the civil war, José Figueres was installed as president of a temporary ruling junta, or council. He called this body the Founding Junta of the Second Republic, to contrast it with the "failed" first republic. Figueres agreed that, after an interim period of eighteen months, he would hand over the reins of government to the elected president, Otilio Ulate. During the brief period that it governed, the junta executed emergency decrees, nationalized the banks, and established a tax on wealth to help pay for repairs necessitated by the war. It extended voting rights to women and streamlined the system of Social Guarantees set up by Calderón.

Figueres also established an electoral system that eliminated the traditional system of political patronage to gain office and established the modern Costa Rican democracy in which political parties compete in fair and honest elections and then peacefully transfer power from one administration to the next.

The junta confronted repeated counterrevolutionary threats from supporters of Calderón, who were known as *calderonistas* (kahl-day-ron-NEES-tahs). In an effort to ward off a military coup, Figueres abolished the Costa Rican army in December 1948. He replaced it with the Civil Guard, made up of approximately 1,500 men led by loyal officers from his own National Liberation Army. For added protection, Figueres signed the Río Treaty, a regional pact for mutual defense in case of attack against a national government. The United States was also a party to the treaty.

The 1949 constitution drawn up by Figueres abolished the military. He explained the move by drawing an analogy. If a family member was ill, he said, the doctor would make a house call. But after that person recovered, there was no need for the doctor to live with the family for the rest of his life.

The new constitution was adopted in 1949 by an elected constituent assembly. It was the ninth constitution since 1825 and continues to serve as the foundation for the Costa Rican government. In addition to separating the executive, legislative, and judicial powers of government, it also established the Supreme Electoral Tribunal that controls the electoral process and supervises the Civil Registry. It prohibits a permanent army and the formation of any political party with ties to an international movement, effectively outlawing any Communist Party. The 1949 constitution includes the Social Guarantees established under Calderón.

In a new constitution, drawn up by Figueres in 1949, the country's military was abolished, a point of national pride today.

DON PEPE On November 8, 1949, Figueres and the other members of the ruling junta handed the reins of government over to Ulate and the Legislative Assembly as promised. Figueres was later hailed as "the grandfather of modern Costa Rica." He was affectionately called Don Pepe by the Costa Rican populace (Pepe is a common nickname for José). In 1951, Figueres founded the National Liberation Party (PLN) and announced his candidacy for president in the 1953 elections. The PLN was founded with the support of the middle class, and it included business and agricultural interests. Don Pepe was elected in a landslide victory and went on to preside over what became a controversial presidential term. Public spending soared as he increased the number of public employees, raised the minimum wage, and increased public expenditure on education and housing.

Figueres and the controversial president of Nicaragua, Anastasio Somoza García, had a deep personal dislike of each other and often supported each other's opponents in exile. In January 1955, hundreds of well-armed calderonistas invaded Costa Rica from across the Nicaraguan border and captured the town of Quesada. Figueres sought help from the United States under the Río Treaty. The Organization of American States ordered both countries to disassociate themselves from insurgent military forces in each other's territories. The two governments signed a formal treaty of friendship in December 1956, but border conflicts continued to flare up occasionally. Figueres was voted out of office in 1957 in favor of the Republican Party (PR), which carried on the calderonista legacy. The new president was unable to lower the large national debt, however, and the PLN recaptured power in the 1962 elections. This pattern was repeated over the next several elections, as the PLN alternately won and lost the presidency.

POLITICAL AND ECONOMIC CRISES

The 1980s were characterized by political and military conflicts throughout the region. The US Central Intelligence Agency established a base in Costa Rica from which to attack Sandinistas in Nicaragua, despite opposition from the US Congress. Many Nicaraguans sought refuge from the violence in Costa Rica, which added to tensions between Costa Ricans and Nicaraguans. The Costa Rican government also faced rising opposition at home. Once again, the PLN's opponent was unable to reduce the external debt, and the PLN was voted back into power in the 1982 elections. By imposing austerity measures, the administration was able to pull the country out of the worst of its economic crisis. The PLN was reelected in 1986, installing Óscar Arias Sánchez as president.

Arias found himself obliged to prolong many of the austerity measures of the previous administration in order to revive the economy. He also helped bring an end to the regional political crisis. After nearly a decade of warfare in Nicaragua and El Salvador, Arias drafted a regional peace accord that proposed to end hostilities and to bring democracy to the war-torn countries. The five Central American presidents signed the accord on August 7, 1987. The Arias plan succeeded where other attempts had failed, largely because it was designed and agreed upon by the Central American governments themselves. President Arias was awarded the Nobel Peace Prize in 1987 for his role in the peace process.

Nonetheless, protests by labor unions and public employees mounted again during the late 1980s. The PLN lost the presidential and legislative elections in 1990, yielding power to Rafael Ángel Calderón Fournier, the son of Rafael Ángel Calderón Guardia, who represented the Social Christian Unity Party (PUSC). Public dissatisfaction with the continued economic austerity measures helped the PLN to regain the presidency in 1994, represented by José María Figueres Olsen, the son of Don Pepe Figueres. The PLN did not win a majority in the Legislative Assembly, however. Although the presidency subsequently went to the PUSC, in 2006 Arias was installed as president for the PLN for a second term.

In 2010, Laura Chinchilla Miranda, a member of the PLN, became the first female president of Costa Rica. She served until 2014. A former historian and diplomat, Luis Guillermo Solís Rivera, was her successor. Solís ran as part of the Citizen Action Party (PAC). He remains president as of 2017.

Laura Chinchilla Miranda was elected the first woman president of Costa Rica in 2010.

INTERNET LINKS

http://www.biography.com/people/simon-bolivar-241196
Biography.com has detailed information on historical figures, such as Simón Bolívar.

https://www.britannica.com/place/Costa-Rica
The Encyclopedia Britannica's website provides historical information on Costa Rica.

http://globaledge.msu.edu/countries/costa-rica
Global Edge, hosted by Michigan State University, provides historical information on Costa Rica.

GOVERNMENT

The historic Legislative Assembly building in San José is the seat of Costa Rica's parliament.

3

S AN JOSÉ IS THE SEAT OF government in Costa Rica, which boasts the oldest democratic republic in the region. Costa Rica is characterized by regular and fair elections, a literate and politically active population, and a focus on human rights and freedoms. Their focus on the environment and personal freedoms has led the country to abolish the nation's military. Every four years, on the first Sunday in February, Costa Rican citizens over eighteen years old elect their national officials. These positions include the president, two vice presidents, members of the Legislative Assembly, and local members of the municipal councils.

In 2016, the Legatum Prosperity Index put Costa Rica in the world's top thirty most prosperous countries, and in the top twenty countries for personal freedom.

NATIONAL GOVERNMENT

Costa Rica's national government is divided into three branches: executive, legislative, and judicial. There is also the Supreme Electoral Tribunal, which is almost a fourth branch in that it functions as a completely independent part of the government. Prior to the 1940s, the Costa Rican government tried to limit its role in the economy. Since the presidency of Rafael Ángel Calderón Guardia in the early 1940s, however, the government has intervened in the economy to the extent that its leaders have considered necessary in order to provide social benefits to the citizens. The government's hand in the economy is felt through its system of nationalized banking, petroleum refineries, and utilities. Social welfare priorities include public education and health and public assistance programs. Thus, in 1990, the United Nations declared Costa Rica to have the best human development index among underdeveloped countries. By 1992, Costa Rica was removed from the list of underdeveloped countries.

FOUNDATIONS AND REGULATIONS

The modern republic is founded upon the 1949 constitution, which prohibits the president and legislators from being elected to more than one term in succession. It guarantees political rights for women and the right to a minimum wage for all citizens.

The Supreme Electoral Tribunal calls for the country's elections and controls the electoral process. It also supervises the Civil Registry, which issues identity cards, draws up voter lists, and records births, deaths, marriages, and naturalization. The Supreme Court of Justice appoints magistrates to the tribunal through a two-thirds vote, at staggered intervals so that the body always has a mixture of fresh perspectives and maturity.

Until the 1940s political parties were formed primarily around the personal political ambitions of a single candidate. After the 1948 civil war, the National Liberation Party (PLN) emerged as a party that attempted to represent a well-defined political platform. Nevertheless, the PLN continued to be identified with its founder, José Figueres, until his death in 1990, after which his son, José María Figueres, picked up the banner and announced immediately that he was running for president.

The Social Christian Unity Party (PUSC) is a coalition of four major groups: the Republican Calderonista Party, Democratic Renovation Party, Popular Unity Party, and Christian Democratic Party. For many years, it was the strongest opposition party, alternating in power with the PLN since 1948, under different names and in various combinations. In 2000, though, the Citizen Action Party (PAC) was formed and quickly became a strong presidential election contender. Today, the current president, Luis Guillermo Solís, is a member of the PAC.

EXECUTIVE BRANCH The president heads the executive branch with the assistance of two vice presidents, and the Council of Government. The presidential candidate must receive at least 40 percent of the vote to win the election, after which he or she serves in office for four years. Voting is not just available to all citizens in Costa Rica; it is compulsory, or mandatory, for all citizens, leading to a very politically active society.

The Costa Rican coat of arms was originally designed in 1848 and was last updated in 1998.

The president appoints cabinet ministers, who do not need to be approved by congress, and these cabinet members focus on specific areas of policy, such as education or the environment. Some of the primary responsibilities of the president include representing the country in official acts and commanding the public security forces.

LEGISLATIVE BRANCH Costa Rica has a unicameral Legislative Assembly composed of fifty-seven members. Deputies are elected for four-year terms, which may not be repeated successively. A deputy must be a Costa Rican citizen, either by birth or after ten years of naturalization, and must be at least twenty-one years old. The 1949 constitution awards the primary share of power to the Legislative Assembly. This branch holds the exclusive powers to enact or repeal laws, approve the national budget, levy taxes, and authorize the president to declare a national state of emergency. The Legislative Assembly may approve or reject international treaties and loans, appoint magistrates of the Supreme Court of Justice, and form new courts.

The Costa Rican Supreme Electoral Tribunal protects the nation's elections and democratic processes.

JUDICIAL BRANCH Members of the Supreme Court of Justice are nominated by the Legislative Assembly every eight years. The court rules over the country's judicial system and is divided into three chambers. The first chamber deals with appeals against administrative, civil, and commercial judgments made by the lower courts. The second chamber considers appeals against lower-court judgments on family issues, conflicts of jurisdiction between judicial and administrative authorities, and other matters. The third chamber considers criminal appeals, claims of injury and libel, and other matters relating to the criminal justice system.

LOCAL GOVERNMENT

Costa Rica is divided administratively into provinces, cantons, and districts. There are seven provinces, but these have little administrative power. Rather, they serve primarily to partition the country into judicial and electoral jurisdictions. The president appoints governors to oversee the provinces, but their responsibilities are limited.

NATIONAL SECURITY

Costa Rica prides itself on having no standing military. In fact, its citizens grow indignant at the slightest hint of militarism. Even at the height of regional political instability in the 1980s, Costa Ricans strongly opposed any response that included increased national militarism. Conversely, Costa Ricans resent any attempt by foreign powers to dominate them. During the regional political crisis of the 1980s, Costa Rica withstood pressures to follow the United States in its war against Nicaragua, despite US sanctions on economic aid and diplomatic relations.

Instead, Costa Ricans take pride in their country's image as an oasis of tranquility. The enforcement of law and order rests on the police, and on air and naval communications, drug control, and intelligence units.

In 1969, a constitutional amendment prohibited the president from serving more than once in a lifetime. In 2003, however, this was overturned, and now second presidential terms are allowed, provided the terms aren't consecutive.

INTERNET LINKS

https://www.cia.gov/library/publications/the-world-factbook/geos/cs.html
The World Factbook, hosted by the Central Intelligence Agency, is full of information on the governments of countries all over the world, including Costa Rica.

http://www.costarica-embassy.org/index.php?q=node/21
The website for the Embassy of Costa Rica has information about the country's government and laws.

ECONOMY

Costa Rica's money, the colón, is colorful and decorated with rich illustrations.

4

THANKS IN PART TO THEIR FOCUS ON international peace and low military spending, Costa Rica has one of the largest per capita incomes, and the highest standard of living, among its Central American neighbors.

FACTS AND FIGURES

A nation's economy relies on a wide range of factors, including domestic education, innovation, and foreign trade. The total value of a country's goods and services is called the gross domestic product (GDP). Typically, a high GDP means higher incomes for individuals in that country. Of course, not everyone makes the same amount, and wealth and income inequality can develop, which has been the case in Costa Rica.

In 2016, Costa Rica's GDP was $79 billion—a huge increase from $19.4 billion in 2005. This is roughly equivalent to $15,400 per person, and it reflects a consistent annual growth rate of 2 to 4 percent over the past ten years. The rate of inflation, or rate at which a currency loses value, has been fairly consistent, around 5 percent each year since 2009. While Costa Rica is relatively well off in comparison with other countries in the region, its prospects for economic growth remain hindered by its large public and foreign debt, equivalent to nearly two-thirds of the GDP.

Costa Rica and her neighbors support a free trade agreement with the United States called the Central America—Dominican Republic Free Trade Agreement (CAFTA-DR). Under CAFTA-DR, imports and exports to and from the United States will eventually become tariff free, and

The banana industry may have diversified Costa Rica's exports, but Costa Ricans continue to view coffee as the heart and soul of their economy. Surrounded by the folklore of the small coffee growers, Costa Ricans nostalgically associate the coffee crop with the growth of their democratic tradition.

Coffee was introduced near the end of the eighteenth century. By 1829, it was the country's primary source of foreign exchange. It was vigorously promoted by dictator Braulio Carrillo Colina and President José María Castro Madriz. Carrillo offered free land to anyone who agreed to plant coffee, and he constructed roads for transporting the harvested beans to market.

By the mid-1800s, a small group of prosperous coffee growers, although only modestly wealthy in comparison with other Latin American elites, was able to influence the government to keep taxes low and to promote the coffee trade. Fortunately, this politically powerful elite did not use its influence to oppress the underclass. Rather, the government enacted policies to develop education and public works, in the belief that an educated and well-off populace would lead to greater progress and prosperity for all. This enlightened self-interest inspired the coffee barons to reinvest the profits of their international trade, financing improvements within Costa Rica.

American companies in Central America will be treated like local companies. The hope of the CAFTA-DR is to bring about economic growth and stability for small but independent countries like Costa Rica.

While Costa Rica has seen overall economic improvement, the country has been struggling with economic inequality for many years. For more than twenty years, 25 percent of the population has been below the poverty line, while one-tenth of the population still lives in absolute poverty, where people do not have access to basic necessities such as food, water, and shelter.

ECONOMIC SETBACKS

For nearly two decades, Costa Rica suffered from economic constraints, which severely compromised efforts to maintain a strong system of social benefits. The national debt increased year after year to pay for social welfare programs. A shortfall in revenues was caused in part by a sharp decline in international coffee prices and exports. By 1981, the country's foreign debt had risen to $3 billion, and Costa Rica's total debt per person was the fourth highest in the world. Inflation was more than 50 percent, and unemployment had soared to nearly 10 percent.

In September 1981, the government was so far behind in interest payments on its foreign debt that it announced it was going to stop servicing the debt and requested that payments be rescheduled. Costa Rica thus became the first underdeveloped country to suspend debt payments, although a wave of such actions followed during the worldwide economic recession of the early 1980s. The International Monetary Fund (IMF), the World Bank, and the US Agency for International Development agreed to lend Costa Rica money to meet its most pressing financial needs and to make up for revenue loss caused

As development and modernization continue across the country, rural farmers struggle to keep up economically.

by declining coffee exports. They did this because the various organizations were anxious to avert any political consequences that might befall the only stable democracy in an otherwise volatile region.

These organizations stipulated several conditions, including the requirement that the government devalue the Costa Rican currency, reduce public spending, lift price controls on gasoline and public utility charges, privatize several state agencies, and reform the tax system to improve methods of collection. By the early 1990s, Costa Rica seemed to have resumed a slow economic recovery. The rate of increase in per-capita income rose from 1 percent in 1990 to 7.7 percent by 1992. Nonetheless, from 2000 to 2004 the rate of increase dropped to around 1 percent before regaining significant ground in 2005.

Since 2005, Costa Rica has seen a dramatic improvement in the average per-capita income, but the wealth gap continues to grow due to a number of factors. First is the gap in education between the poor and wealthy. It's estimated that the poverty rate would be cut in half if Costa Ricans without a high school diploma earned as much as those who graduated. Another way to confront this is to focus on education itself and encourage all citizens to finish high school. Second, while Costa Rica has been more prosperous than other Latin American countries, it has also seen an increase in its cost of living. This is compounded when immigrants, primarily from Nicaragua, move to Costa Rica looking for higher wages, find they cannot meet the higher cost of living, and become dependent on Costa Rica's robust social welfare system. Finally, the country's economic improvements have largely come from exporting goods, which benefits large businesses that produce enough to send to foreign countries. Domestically, however, local businesses face high taxes and high prices with little improvement to their own incomes.

EXPORTS AND ASSETS

Costa Rica relies heavily on its exports for economic development. Bananas, coffee, sugar, and livestock have long been the country's traditional exports. But new agricultural products as well as nonagricultural products have been introduced to the country, increasing industrial activity and exports.

Agriculture and livestock are a major part of Costa Rica's economy, but the economic profile is changing. Nontraditional agricultural export products (export crops or products introduced into a region where they had not been grown or harvested before) have risen tremendously during the past few decades. These exports include flowers, ornamental plants and foliage, fresh and frozen fish, shrimp, melons, macadamia nuts, and pineapples. Unfortunately for Costa Rican farmers, most of the nontraditional export trade, with the exception of fish, is controlled by foreign-owned companies that have better access to technology and marketing strategies and take most of the profit. Other major crops include cocoa, cotton, and hemp.

Foreign-owned companies benefiting from Costa Rica's fertile land and long growing season might mean a modern twist on the "banana republic."

In the 1950s, 50 percent of the labor force worked in agriculture, turning out 95 percent of total exports. Industry contributed only 13 percent of the gross domestic product. In 2015, agriculture was closer to 5.6 percent of the GDP and 14 percent of the labor force, while industry contributed to nearly 20 percent of the GDP.

Farmers are able to produce a wide variety of crops because of the range of climates in the country. Besides export crops, they also cultivate crops for domestic consumption. These include beans, corn, plantains, potatoes, rice, sorghum (a grain similar to corn), onions, and African palms, from which they derive palm oil. Farmers also raise livestock for the domestic market, including cattle, pigs, horses, mules, sheep, goats, and chickens.

The forests are generally viewed as obstacles to progress, and timber is often burned or left to rot. There is no formal system of reforestation, and most developers and landless peasants do not see the need for such a program. Despite this bleak picture, Costa Rica is internationally renowned for its efforts to conserve its natural environment. The government has set aside a quarter of the land area for national parks, forest reserves, indigenous reservations, and wildlife refuges. The legislature has also passed laws to protect Costa Rica's land, water, and forests—although the laws are often disregarded by developers.

INDUSTRY

With membership in the Central American Common Market, Costa Rica has increased its industrial production, and with government assistance in high-tech industries, more people are seeking jobs in urban areas. The sectors of industry, information technology, and tourism have gained increasing dominance in the economy.

Costa Rica produces a wide variety of light manufactured goods. While food, beverages, and tobacco have traditionally been the main manufacturing activities, medical equipment, electronics, pharmaceuticals, and software development have become key industries in recent years.

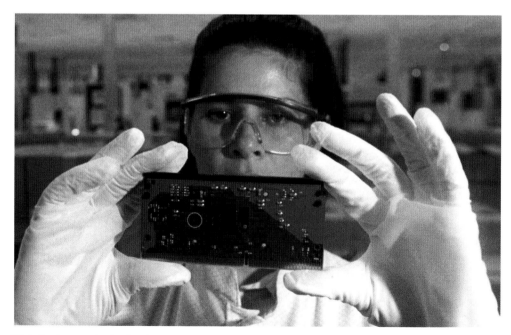

High-tech manufacturing is a growing industry in Costa Rica.

Other manufactured goods include rubber, plastics, chemicals, textiles, adhesives, cosmetics, bricks and cement, fertilizer, and wood products.

Mining consists primarily of the extraction of nonmetallic minerals such as limestone, sand, salt, and clay. Gold is mined in small amounts, though large mining companies have been banned because of the environmental damages caused by the practice.

Intensified interest by international firms in conducting oil exploration on Costa Rican soil prompted the government in 2002 to take a firm environmental stand and prohibit all oil exploration. In 2011, President Laura Chinchilla placed another moratorium, or pause, on oil explorations, and in 2014, President Luis Guillermo Solís extended this ban until 2021. An oil pipeline does, however, carry imported crude oil to a refinery at Moín, where the oil is redistributed to the highlands and other regions of Costa Rica.

Hydroelectric power provides the primary source of electrical energy. With its abundant rainfall and favorable terrain, Costa Rica has enormous hydroelectric potential, and about a dozen hydroelectric plants have been built on various rivers. Other energy sources include diesel and gas turbine generation for electricity, as well as the burning of wood, charcoal, and bagasse (vegetable waste, primarily from sugarcane).

TOURISM

Costa Rica broke its national record for most tourists in 2015, with 2.6 million visitors. This is in keeping with the country's steady stream of visitors—more than 2 million annually since 2008. In 2013, Costa Rica made nearly $6 billion from tourism alone, 12 percent of the country's GDP that year. Tourism accounted for 12 percent of the country's jobs.

With its abundance of natural beauty, ecotourism in Costa Rica is booming. Indeed, tourism has become one of the country's primary sources of revenue, surpassing the export earnings of both bananas and coffee combined.

The most popular destinations for tourists include natural wonders as well as cultural and historical sites. One attraction is the Arenal volcano, which was active until 2010. It offers hot springs, zip lines, rafting, and hiking. The most devastating eruption in the volcano's history buried three small villages

and killed 87 people, but today the volcano is appreciated for its geothermal activity, which heats springs and provides a natural hot tub. The Manuel Antonio National Park draws tourists with its beaches, rain forests, and diverse wildlife. The park is home to 109 species of mammals and 184 species of birds, and lucky visitors to small islands off the coast can catch a glimpse of dolphins and migrating whales.

Tourism to Costa Rica's vibrant coasts and luscious rain forests provides an important source of income for the country.

In the capital of San José, the Museum of Contemporary Art and Design is noted for its large collection of over nine hundred works in a wide array of mediums. The museum focuses on artists from Central America, whose works relate to life in the region. Only 8 miles (13 km) away, in Heredia, visitors are attracted to the historical structure of the Iglesia de la Inmaculada Concepción. Constructed in 1736, this church was originally built by colonists to convert natives to Catholicism. Though the church is modest in many ways, it is adorned with twenty stained-glass windows from France.

The services sector is the largest area of the economy, generating 75 percent of the country's GDP. Services include social, financial, communal, and personal services in occupational areas such as transportation, health care, restaurants and hotels, communications, real estate, and insurance.

TRANSPORTATION AND COMMUNICATIONS

Improved transportation and communications have linked all parts of the country and opened it up tremendously during the last few decades. The Meseta Central, or Central Valley, serves as the hub of the transportation system. The major highways and railroads extend from there to the Pacific and Caribbean lowlands. Transportation systems include railroads, international air travel, inland waterways, and roads for the country's increased number of cars and buses. The Pan-American Highway runs the length of the country, from the Nicaraguan border to Panama. Inland waterways act as important conduits for communication, cargo, and passengers in the north and northeastern parts of the country. Two important routes are the San Carlos and Sarapiquí Rivers, both of which flow northward through the plains.

Communication systems in Costa Rica include the telegraph, telephone, radio, television, the internet, newspapers, and several periodicals. In 2004, about 90 percent of households had a television, and about one in every three people owned a telephone or mobile phone. Today, there are 144 mobile phone subscriptions per 100 people—more than one phone per person. Because telecommunications companies now bundle media— internet, phone, and television—it is difficult to estimate exactly how many homes have a television or use a computer to serve the same purpose. Between 2000 and 2015, internet usage jumped from less than 6 percent to nearly 60 percent.

INTERNET LINKS

http://www.focus-economics.com/countries/costa-rica
Focus Economics is run by economic experts who predict trends around the world.

http://data.worldbank.org/country/costa-rica
The World Bank works to end poverty and has information on the economy of many countries, including Costa Rica.

ENVIRONMENT

Costa Ricans are protective of their country's natural beauty and resources.

5

● ● ● ● ● ● ● ● ● ● ● ● ●
In 2008, the Costa Rican government outlined a plan to have the country be entirely carbon neutral by 2021. In 2015, however, they extended their deadline to 2085.

COSTA RICA ENJOYS RENEWABLE energy and an active tourism industry thanks to a rich, environmentally diverse landscape. The government is committed to preserving the country's natural beauty and resources through a system of national parks, and the small country has received numerous international awards for its conservation efforts.

NATURAL PROTECTION

Costa Rica is often ranked in the top five "eco-friendly" countries in the world. Nevertheless, the country still struggles with environmental protection. Its conservation laws are often violated, and the nation still experiences rapid deforestation, especially outside the national parks and reserves.

The Nature Conservancy, an international organization whose mission it is to preserve flora and fauna by protecting their habitats, conducted a survey among Costa Ricans in 2005 that revealed most Costa Ricans are as concerned about environmental problems, such as air and water pollution, as they are about crime rates and public health services. While the government seems to be doing many things right (Costa Rica complies with many environmental treaties), having achieved one of the

Many economic factors led to massive deforestation across Costa Rica.

best conservation records in the world, it still has some way to go in other areas that affect the quality of life for average Costa Ricans.

DEFORESTATION

With Costa Rica's world-class achievements in conservation, it might be surprising to learn that by the 1990s much of the country had been deforested. In fact, Costa Rica once had one of the worst deforestation rates in Central America, with forests being felled at an alarming rate of more than 193 square miles (500 sq km) annually. Those numbers have improved, however, and the rate of deforestation has slowed to 31 square miles (80 sq km) annually. In the 1960s, the United States offered Costa Rican ranchers millions of dollars in loans to stimulate beef production, which led to massive deforestation. In addition, the growing population continually exerts pressure on the government to clear land for human habitation. However, efforts were taken in the 1990s to replenish forest areas. As of 2011, the country has 52 percent forest cover.

The effects of deforestation are long lasting, however. It has resulted in many animal and plant species becoming endangered. With no forest cover to protect the land, the soil is exposed to the sun and the rain, leaving it thin, dry, and easy to erode. Natural water sources such as rivers and streams have also been affected, becoming more prone to flooding or drying up.

To stem the rate of deforestation, the government initiated innovative forest protection programs to promote sustainable development. One such program involved a forest management plan for landowners, entitling them to payment for every acre of forest protected. The government also tried to promote reforestation through tax incentives. While deforestation rates have dropped, the remaining forests are still threatened by illegal logging.

TRADING RAIN FORESTS FOR GREENHOUSE GASES

Greenhouse gases are atmospheric gases such as carbon dioxide (CO_2) and methane, which contribute to global warming. Forests provide a natural protection from increased greenhouse gas emissions because trees take in CO_2 and produce oxygen, a necessity for human life. When forests are cut down, however, not only is CO_2 left to enter the atmosphere, but rotting trees left after a forest has been cleared release additional greenhouse gasses. It is estimated that 20 to 30 percent of global emissions are due to deforestation.

At a UN summit on climate change in 2005, Costa Rica was part of a coalition of ten developing countries that successfully proposed a deal for wealthy nations to compensate poor nations for tropical rain forest conservation. The deal is based on the preservation of forests in developing countries as a counter to greenhouse gas emissions in wealthy countries prospering from urbanization. It is hoped that slowing deforestation will help slow climate change.

In a move toward putting this plan into action, in 2013 President Laura Chinchilla and the Costa Rican government signed an Emissions Reduction Agreement worth $63 million, making Costa Rica the first nation to collect large payments for conservation efforts. That money will ultimately go to landowners as incentives to help reforestation efforts, and to protect the trees and habitats already there.

NATIONAL PARKS AND CONSERVATION

In 1970, Costa Rica established its greatly admired national park system, covering all of the country's major ecosystems and habitats. There are currently twenty-seven national parks managed by the Ministry of Environment and Energy (MINAE). It is responsible for 163 protected areas total. Apart from the national parks, these include biological reserves, forest reserves, wildlife refuges, wetlands, mangroves, and marine areas. Together, the protected areas cover approximately one-quarter of Costa Rica and provide a safe haven for about 75 percent of the country's species of flora and fauna.

In 1998, MINAE established eleven regional conservation areas, which are known as Sistema Nacional de Áreas de Conservación (National System of Conservation Areas), or SINAC. As part of this system, several parks, private

Land conservation is also wildlife conservation, as natural habitats provide shelter to countless species of exotic animals.

conservation areas, and other protected zones have been joined together and now encompass complete and unique ecosystems. The aim is to provide larger areas in which wildlife can migrate and move around. The conservation areas are Arenal Huetar Norte, Arenal Tilarán, Caribbean La Amistad, Pacific La Amistad, Central Volcanic Cordillera, Central Pacific, Guanacaste, Osa, Tempisque, Tortuguero, and Cocos Island Marine.

Costa Rica also has many conservation groups that have taken on various roles and responsibilities, from managing private nature reserves to setting up forest management projects. Efforts have also been made to involve local communities by integrating their livelihoods into the day-to-day operation of the national park system. The purpose of this is to teach locals that it is possible to earn a living by preserving rather than destroying the environment.

Ecotourism, the practice of visiting natural habitats or attractions with as little impact to the environment as possible, is a booming business in Costa Rica. On the surface, that appears to be a good thing. Attracting more visitors to the parks means more revenue and more job opportunities. There are concerns in some quarters, however, that Costa Rica's ecotourism drive could actually end up damaging the ecology as developers clear land to construct new hotels and facilities that cater to growing waves of tourists. The challenge for the government is to balance the demands of the ecotourism industry with long-term conservation needs.

WASTE MANAGEMENT

While Costa Rica's conservation system is idealistic, its water and waste management systems are still lacking. Almost all Costa Ricans have access to a water supply source, but the water is not always safe to drink. Tourism has

Costa Rica's ambitious plan to be carbon neutral by 2021 was postponed to 2085, but the country is still committed to environmental policies, and with good reason. In addition to protecting natural beauty and the income it generates in tourism, Costa Rica's location between two oceans makes it vulnerable to sea level rise and other impacts of global warming.

In September 2015, the country released its Intended Nationally Determined Contribution (INDC) report, outlining the nation's plan for reduced emissions. Rather than 2021 marking the end of emissions, it has become the turning point at which Costa Rica will begin a more robust plan to mitigate carbon emissions. This includes regular goals for reduction, beginning with 1.73 net tons per capita in 2030, which will accompany a use of 100 percent renewable energy (the country currently gets 8.8 percent of electricity from imported oil), and increased efficiency in households and businesses. By 2050, emissions should have dropped to 1.19 tons per capita, and finally reach 0 emissions in 2085. To reach these goals, new environmental policies focus on forest conservation, agriculture innovations, renewable energy, transportation, and waste management.

While reforestation helps to absorb emissions, agricultural technologies are needed to address the adverse effects of livestock—including methane gases, and water waste and runoff. Improved transportation efficiency wouldn't just help the environment but would also provide better air quality for residents, as well as improved routes and better commute times. According to the INDC report, the country's third-largest contributor to emissions is solid waste, such as construction waste. To address this growing issue, urban planning commissions are working with the Ministry of Health to improve garbage sorting, recycling, and composting programs.

The new plan even includes hopes that in 2100, the country will produce negative emissions, where their efforts could negate 0.27 tons per capita of emissions from other countries.

further strained the limited water supply as new hotels and resorts demand more water for guests.

There is also limited sewage treatment in Costa Rica, including San José. As late as 2015, 98 percent of Costa Ricans had access to an improved drinking source, but only 15 percent of black water was treated. The rest was dumped in rivers and oceans. Additionally, high levels of wastewater in water companies—some above 50 percent—represent the exact kind of inefficiencies the government is trying to combat in its attempt to go green.

The country produces 2,400 tons (2,177 metric tons) of solid waste annually, with 60 percent going to open dumps, 15 percent to landfills, and less than 10 percent getting recycled. It is estimated that 300 additional tons (272 metric tons) of waste are dumped in streets and rivers, causing flooding and contaminating water sources.

But the situation is not hopeless. In 2010, the government passed Ley 8839, a law targeted at improving waste management at all stages, from production to consumer, and emphasizing citizens' role in properly disposing waste. On the industrial level, the National Recycling Strategy began planning in 2016 for a platform where industries could sell their reusable and recyclable waste, incentivizing reducing waste and improving recycling.

Some areas in particular have experienced the disastrous consequences of the lack of a decent sewage system. At one point, practically all of the sewage from the highly populated Central Valley was pumped untreated into the Río Grande de Tárcoles. The town of Tárcoles on the Pacific coast faced a desperate situation. Once a popular destination for tourists, it was given a wide berth, as the river running through it reeked and bubbled with sewage. Ironically, tourists still traveled the river itself, as it boasted an enormous crocodile population.

Things changed for the area in the early 2000s, however, when the government announced a plan to clean the river by building a wastewater treatment plant in San José. In 2015, the Los Trajos wastewater treatment facility finally opened. The first of its size in the region, it has the capacity to handle the sewage generated by about 65 percent of the Central Valley population.

DRINKING WATER AND MARINE LIFE

Water may be the most abundant resource on Earth, but pollution and salination both play a role in ruining it for humans and wildlife alike. Waste and pollutants from urban centers in Costa Rica flow into its rivers and into the ocean, which has had a devastating effect on marine life. This can be seen along the shorelines and coral reefs, and in the death of marine life such as fish, turtles, and dolphins. The Caribbean shorelines are also clogged with soil deposits washed into the waterways as a result of deforestation and natural disasters. In addition, the indiscriminate dumping of industrial waste from ships at sea damages the fragile marine ecosystem.

City waste is rarely disposed of properly, causing it to enter waterways and negatively impact marine life.

In the early 1990s, local residents of Puerto Viejo, a village near the Caribbean coast, ran out of potable water. The river water that they were accustomed to drinking had become polluted with sewage and garbage. Their search for clean water elsewhere prompted a research biologist at the Universidad Nacional Autonoma de Costa Rica, Dr. Claudia Charpentier, who had been studying the waterways in that area, to include community outreach in her project. She developed the Water for Life program, an environmental education program focused on water quality and quantity in the lowlands of Costa Rica. Graduate students, educators, and local community leaders got involved in developing teaching materials to help villagers understand the connection between the environment, human activities, and clean drinking water. The aim is to empower them with the knowledge of how to safeguard their local water sources.

AGRICULTURAL IMPACT

While Costa Rica's main traditional agricultural products—bananas and coffee—have provided a foundation for economic growth, the environment has paid a price. For example, large tracts of land have been deforested in

Even with Costa Rica's excellent farming conditions, the use of chemical pesticides and herbicides can be devastating to people, wildlife, and the crops themselves, leading to waste and pollution.

order to make way for banana plantations. Furthermore, today's cultivation is also marked by the high use of pesticides and fertilizers, which can have negative effects on plants and insects not intended to be treated, as well as humans. Costa Rica has one of the highest rates of pesticide use, more than twice the average used in other parts of the region. Apart from displacing whole communities of wildlife and destroying the biodiversity of flora and fauna, the clearing of forest cover and intense use of pesticides have contaminated much of the soil and reduced it to silt, which gets washed away by the rain into nearby streams and rivers.

Banana plantations also generate vast amounts of waste—double the volume of bananas produced. There are generally two types of waste—biodegradable (organic) and non-biodegradable. Organic waste consists of the shoots, leaves, flowers, and other parts of the banana plant, which are either added back to the soil or thrown into large open-air dumps. Because these plant parts are very fibrous, they may decompose very slowly. As they are often not treated, the risk of bacterial buildup is high, and leaching from the waste may seep into underground water sources.

Non-biodegradable waste includes the plastic bags, containers, and string used to wrap or pack the bananas. Plastic bags are commonly used during the growing period to protect the fruit from insects, and the bags are often impregnated with an insecticide. Although there are laws on pollution control regarding proper treatment of waste, they are not strictly adhered to. While some plantations burn or recycle these bags after use, others throw them into open dumps. They are even found floating in rivers or the sea, polluting the water and affecting river and marine life.

In the case of coffee, the story is much the same. Waste products are dumped into waterways, which is hazardous because the coffee bean contains contaminants that can destroy fauna and harm people. In the 1970s, a new species of coffee plant, called the sun coffee plant, was introduced. It requires much more sunlight and results in a bigger loss of trees and soil erosion. The fruit of the coffee tree is called a cherry. Another environmental problem lies in the process of separating the ripe cherry pulp from its seeds—the coffee beans. After fermenting in a water tank for a day, the pulp is separated from the beans, which are set out in the sun to dry. The sugared water from the pulp drains into rivers, starving aquatic life of oxygen and depleting it.

Though Costa Rica is proud of its rich natural resources and biodiversity, the nation struggles to balance development and industry with its goals of environmental sustainability. Often it is the country's greatest assets—such as tourism to its ecological wonders—which threaten those very resources.

To the surprise of environmental groups, the Costa Rican government has agreed to remove its protection of endangered and threatened shark species. The benefit, the government hopes, will be a short-term increase in wages for fishermen struggling to get by. The lasting repercussions, however, may be an incalculable cost to the environment.

INTERNET LINKS

http://www.nature.org/ourinitiatives/regions/centralamerica/costarica
This article discusses conservation efforts in Costa Rica.

http://www.worldwatch.org/node/4958
This article discusses Costa Rica's plans to go carbon neutral.

COSTA RICANS

With many influences throughout the country's history, the people of Costa Rica are varied and pride themselves on their unique culture.

6

Costa Rica has long served as a sanctuary for exiles from other countries—from Central American and Eastern European refugees escaping political persecution to drug lords and arms traffickers fleeing criminal prosecution.

COSTA RICANS AFFECTIONATELY refer to themselves as *ticos* (TEE-kohs) and pride themselves on their unique culture. They identify firstly as Costa Ricans and secondly as Latin or Central Americans. They often explain certain actions or behavior by saying, "We ticos are like that," and proudly speak of their "idiosyncrasy" or "national reality," which they perceive to be unique.

DIVERSITY

In terms of diversity, Costa Rica represents many nations. The majority of Costa Ricans have Spanish ancestry, but there are others of African descent living in the country as well. Oftentimes, those of African descent face discrimination and isolation from national culture. This is a problem that needs to be examined and improved.

Given the relatively small indigenous population at the time of the Spanish conquest, most indigenous people were either quickly absorbed into the Hispanic population or marginalized in isolated areas. The term "mestizo" was used to distinguish those of mixed indigenous and European ancestry for only a short while. It was not long before most mestizos called themselves "white."

Despite the hardships indigenous populations faced at the hands of the Spanish, there are still vibrant native communities in Costa Rica today.

Approximately 90 percent of the 4.8 million Costa Rican population is white or mestizo, 2.4 percent of the population is indigenous, about 1 percent of the Costa Rican populace is black, and 1 percent is Chinese. Ethnic conflict is limited in Costa Rica, in part because ticos tend to shun conflict but more likely because minorities are such a small percentage of the population. Most mestizos are descended from the Spanish and the Chorotega tribes. They speak a slightly different Spanish dialect from the rest of the highland population. Within this homogenous society, however, certain cultural traditions can be distinguished. In addition to the indigenous and the Spanish-American traditions, one can also observe distinct cultural traditions.

INDIGENOUS PEOPLES

Besides those with mixed indigenous and European ancestry, the remaining indigenous population is very small in relation to the rest of the Costa Rican population. The people prefer to be called *indígenas* (een-DEE-hay-nahs). There are eight ethnic groups, totaling about 104,000 people. Most live near the southern border and work as subsistence farmers.

The largest indigenous group is the Talamanca, a name given to the Bribri and Cabécar peoples who live a rather isolated existence on either side of the Cordillera de Talamanca. Together they make up roughly two-thirds of the total indigenous population. Their pre-Columbian ancestors escaped to this region after the Spanish conquest. The Boruca group, numbering between 1,500 and 2,000, forms another important indigenous population, which lives primarily within three villages in the southwest. Most of them are Spanish speaking.

In the 1960s, the Legislative Assembly created the National Commission of Indian Affairs (CONAI) to improve the social, economic, and cultural situations of the indigenous people and to urge that they be granted the rights and guarantees of full citizenship. Regrettably, this has not yet fully happened. In 1976, the government set aside five land areas for the indigenous population. As of 2007 there were twenty-four reservations. Nonindigenous persons are not allowed to rent, lease, or buy that land, and enforcement of these restrictions has improved in recent years. A fringe benefit of reforestation and forest preservation laws is providing further protection to indigenous populations that live there.

Access to education has also been a challenge for native populations in Costa Rica, and indigenous teachers have complained that they are not hired because preference was given to non-native teachers. Furthermore, despite Costa Rica's long history of funding education, indigenous schools often lack funding for the same resources offered non-native students.

OTHER CULTURES

There are many other communities living in Costa Rica, among them people of African descent as well as people of Chinese descent.

AFRICANS In contrast to many African-American populations in the Western hemisphere, few of Costa Rica's black citizens were not shipped there as slaves. In fact, an 1862 law prohibited the immigration of both blacks and Asians to Costa Rica. When this prohibition was lifted in the late 1800s, many blacks emigrated from Jamaica to work on the Costa Rican railroad project. After the project was completed, many stayed for jobs on the banana plantations.

By the mid-1920s, white Costa Ricans from the Meseta Central began to resent the black banana workers. They charged that the blacks got better jobs in supervisory and clerical positions because they could speak English to the North American supervisors. The whites endeavored to place restrictions

"Banana republic" is a political science term for a small country that is economically dependent on one crop, or significant amounts of foreign investment. The term comes from Latin America's dependence on bananas, often grown on plantations owned by American investors who exploited native labor and destroyed land with unsustainable farming practices.

Black citizens in Costa Rica have had a strong impact on the language, food, and culture of the Caribbean coastal region of the country.

on the movements and rights of blacks. Because the blacks were never allowed to own land, white highlanders found it easy to evict them from the farms they had created in the Caribbean lowlands. Laws prevented them from migrating out of the Caribbean lowlands, and by the 1930s most blacks had been reduced to poverty. Many immigrated to Panama or the United States in search of better opportunities. They were finally given full citizenship rights after the 1948 revolution. Black ticos still tend to be concentrated in the Caribbean coast, however, and they have had a notable influence on the language, culture, and cuisine of Limón province.

CHINESE More than six hundred Chinese laborers came to Costa Rica in 1873 after the prohibition against Asian immigration was briefly lifted to admit railroad workers. The contracts of these Chinese laborers included a provision that they would be sent home as soon as construction was completed. They were paid one-fifth of the normal wage and forced to live and work under miserable conditions. Rather than being returned to China, many of those who survived were sold into household service in the homes of hidalgos.

Today the Chinese population, known as *chinos* (CHEE-nohs), constitutes an important part of Costa Rican society. The first-generation immigrants tended to isolate themselves within their own neighborhoods. Their children, on the other hand, have integrated into the wider community with little difficulty or prejudice. The Chinese tend to distinguish themselves as successful businesspeople, often owning retail stores, restaurants, cinemas, hotels, and bars in some smaller towns.

SOCIETY AND STATUS

Since Costa Rica is relatively homogeneous in terms of ethnicity and culture, divisions within the society are among the social classes, and between rural and urban residents. Most ticos who possess any measure of power, wealth, or status are concentrated in the urban areas of the Meseta Central—especially in San José.

Although they consider it crass to think only of money, most Costa Ricans still perceive wealth as the primary determinant of class position, along with education and occupation. Education is highly valued as the surest route to upward mobility. The government facilitates social and economic opportunity by providing education, pensions, and free health care to its citizens. Nevertheless, inequities in income do exist and recent surveys indicate that the gap between rich and poor may be widening. In 2009, the top 10 percent of society received approximately 40 percent of the national income, while the bottom 10 percent got only 1.2 percent of the total income.

Housing provides a stark example of wealth inequality in Costa Rica.

SOCIOECONOMIC CLASSES

Approximately 25 percent of the population forms the middle class in Costa Rica. Many were children who came from working-class backgrounds but managed to move into the middle class through education. The growth of the public sector has also enabled many people to move into the middle class as bureaucrats. The upper middle class consists of professionals such as doctors, lawyers, and engineers; less wealthy industrialists and merchants; and large landowners without secondary enterprises. They tend to be well educated and may mix with members of the upper class in some social contexts. The lower middle class, on the other hand, consists of white-collar workers, small business owners, and low-salaried professionals such as nurses.

Various elements can be distinguished within the middle class. Mingled among the broad definitions of upper and lower middle class is the conventional middle class, consisting of the bureaucracy and salaried employees.

Though income inequality persists, there is still a middle class in Costa Rica, made up of government and salaried employees.

Members of the middle class may move into the upper class through marriage, by obtaining a professional degree, or by entering politics. The upper class constitutes about 5 percent of the population and consists of two levels: the principal families and the newly rich. The principal families, also called *la societal* (LAH soh-see-eh-TAL) or "the society," correspond to the hidalgos of the colonial era. They are descended from the early gentry and continue to play a strong role in politics.

The lower urban class can be divided into two subgroups, the working class and the marginals. Industrial development in the twentieth century produced a large urban working class, which today forms approximately 50 percent of the population. The working class maintains a reasonably steady income, earning salaries above the minimum wage. The marginals often live below the poverty line. This group includes street vendors, unskilled workers, and domestic servants.

DRESS

Costa Ricans value physical appearance highly; even the poorest ticos strive to present a well-groomed and neat appearance in everyday life. They may skimp on food or other necessities in order to dress stylishly and thus appear as successful as possible. Some may say that clothing is the cheapest status symbol they can buy, since it is easier to obtain than a nice house or luxury car.

Although they always dress neatly, the people do not necessarily always dress formally. Men from the upper and middle classes often put aside their suit coats in favor of short-sleeved shirts with a tie, or even a sport shirt. Young people dress more casually and often wear T-shirts and jeans. Ticos in the Meseta Central do not usually appear in public wearing shorts, which are considered low-class attire.

Overall, Costa Ricans strive for ease in all things. This includes working hard so they can enjoy leisure time during weekends and holidays, as well as a nuanced social etiquette that maintains peace in order to avoid confrontation.

Ticos see fashion as a source of pride, and they make efforts to dress well and comfortably.

INTERNET LINKS

http://www.iwgia.org
The International Work Group for Indigenous Affairs works to improve understanding of indigenous peoples throughout the world.

http://www.travelcostarica.nu
Travel Costa Rica is home to vast information on Costa Rica and the people who live there.

LIFESTYLE

Family and food are central features to a Costa Rican lifestyle.

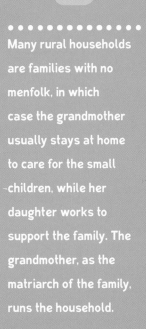

7

COSTA RICANS VALUE THEIR FAMILIES and democratic freedoms above all else. This value system lends itself to a proud nation full of people dedicated to the well-being of their immediate and even distant relatives. Peace and individual rights are so important to ticos that they were able to abolish their military, and the desire to get along trickles down to individual conversations.

ETIQUETTE

Peace is a central value for Costa Ricans, both on a political and personal level. Ticos prefer moderation and compromise over conflict with other people. Rather than committing themselves to a specific position, they are much more likely to hold their opinions in reserve by saying "who knows?" or "perhaps." This reflects their desire for *quedar bien* (kay-DAR bee-EN), or getting along. The saying "Each in his own house and God in all" expresses the same inclination toward harmonious coexistence.

"Quedar bien" is an attitude that governs everyday relations between ticos. It reflects their wish to leave a good impression and to maintain their dignity. It can assume extreme social proportions, however, since the desire for quedar bien often leads people to say things they do not mean or to make promises they do not intend to keep. The immediate

cost of saying "no" is thus avoided in favor of a smiling assent, leaving the rejection for a later time. This does not mean that ticos try to be dishonorable; on the contrary, they simply hope that the moment of disagreeable truth will be indefinitely delayed. For example, promising to do something *mañana*, although literally signifying tomorrow, may mean that they will do it tomorrow, someday, or never. This common social maneuver of saying "yes, but no," helps to avoid friction and thus sustain quedar bien.

Ticos also regard boasting of any kind as vulgar and antisocial. Regardless of social or economic status, they consider it important to act with humility, which enhances their dignity by allowing them to preserve a positive image in front of others. Boasting or pretentiousness of any kind is likely to provoke *choteo* (cho-TAY-oh), or mockery.

The social practice of "quedar bien" is present in all aspects of Costa Rican life and can make facing heated negotiations a challenge, even in diplomacy and politics.

Choteo can range from friendly irony to malicious sarcasm. It also acts as a form of social control, since people fear doing anything that would provoke gossip or ridicule. Although ticos like to think of themselves as individualists, they are not necessarily nonconformists. Social interactions tend to be fairly conservative and highly defined by the values of coexistence and quedar bien. Ticos are quick to gossip about and criticize others but fear becoming the object of choteo themselves.

Ticos value their personal dignity so avidly that extreme forms of choteo can cause legal trouble. Under Costa Rican law, it is illegal to defame someone's honor or impugn the memory of the deceased, since that dishonors the surviving family. Thus politicians must be careful not to attack their opponents on a personal level. On the other hand, ticos tend to be extremely critical of themselves as individuals and as a society.

FRIENDS AND FAMILY

Ticos are strongly oriented toward their own families, villages, and neighborhoods, almost to the exclusion of the larger society or world. They have a traditional saying: "There is no bread like that baked at home."

Personal relations are very important in Costa Rican society. The honor and reputation of the individual and family are carefully protected because the individual depends on his image and personal connections to obtain employment, political advancement, and favors, and even to sidestep legal problems should they arise.

Ticos generally go out of their way to preserve one another's dignity in face-to-face interactions. They treat each other with formal greetings and flowing compliments. In this sense they are a very sociable people and have no problem striking up friendly conversations with strangers.

Although they avoid solitude, Costa Ricans greatly value their privacy. Their surface friendliness masks an inner reserve that often makes them wary of forming intimate friendships outside of their families.

Ticos are social and friendly people, but they are reluctant to form close bonds with people outside their families and communities.

GENDER ROLES

The Costa Ricans' belief in the equality and dignity of all human beings does not necessarily translate into the gender roles they have defined for men and women. From early childhood, girls are taught and expected to be weaker, more emotional, and more vulnerable, and to show less intelligence than boys. Young boys are taught and expected to be more demanding and aggressive than girls and to shine in the classroom.

MACHISMO Men are expected to be daring. They prove their masculinity, or *machismo*, by flirting with women, as well as through exploits such as

Men in Costa Rica are taught to be "macho," or manly. This includes leaving housework to women, catcalling, and shows of strength or courage.

bullfighting and auto racing—or simply by their behavior while driving through traffic. It is not unusual for men to hiss, whistle, or address *piropos* (pee-ROH-pohs), that is, catcalls, to women walking on the street.

Men and boys are taught from an early age to do as they please. Within the family, they generally do not share the responsibility for household chores, and any suggestion of so-called effeminate behavior is ridiculed. Things may be looking up, though, as today's middle-class men are more likely to help their wives around the house.

MARIANISMO For girls, the concept of physical beauty is strongly emphasized. "Queen" contests, or beauty pageants, celebrate feminine beauty for girls and young women in almost every imaginable context. Advertising also perpetuates the sexually attractive feminine ideal. Females learn to receive compliments on their beauty from men and women alike.

Women are expected to serve their husbands and boyfriends, and are responsible for household chores. The feminine ideal of *marianismo* (mah-ree-ahn-EES-moh) demands that women remain loyal, chaste, and submissive, even in the face of a husband's sexual infidelities. Although men are mostly perceived as superior, women are considered to be the stronger sex in moral and spiritual integrity. A woman's virtue is expressed through the sacrifice of her own pleasures for the well-being of her family. One of the highest compliments is for a wife to be described as self-sacrificing.

A Costa Rican woman's reputation and virtue must be protected, and she must carefully avoid becoming an object of gossip. Yet in spite of the social restrictions imposed on women, as many as 50 percent of children are born out of wedlock, and more than 40 percent of poor families are headed by a single mother. This may reflect the perpetual machismo attitude within

Costa Rican culture. In response to this condition, the Law of Fatherhood was passed in 2001 outlining a father's legal obligation to support his children.

Female-headed households are more common among the poor, where fathers abandon their families or the mothers do not sustain long-term relationships. In Costa Rica, living together in a free union without being married is recognized. Such relationships are most common among lower-income couples and in the lowland provinces. Although they lack the social prestige of married couples, men and women in free unions are seldom disparaged, although for women, it is an apparent contradiction of the feminine ideal of virtue and chastity. Women in such open relationships have the same legal rights as wives.

Costa Rican women have been working hard to change their role in society by seeking higher education and entering the workforce.

Children born out of wedlock, called *hijos naturales* (EE-hoes nah-tur-AHL-ays), or "children of nature," are not stigmatized. In cases where their birth is the result of the mother's short-term affair with a man from the middle or upper class, the father will often provide for the support and education of the child. Many upper-class wives, socialized by the ethic of marianismo, tolerate this expense: "After all, it's not the fault of the child."

The traditional role of women has been changing, however, and Costa Rican women are becoming better educated, leading to social liberation. Increasing numbers of middle- and upper-class women are entering the professional, technical, and clerical workforces. Dating without chaperones is also more common than it used to be.

RURAL AND URBAN LIFESTYLES

The contrast between urban and rural living is the basis of economic and social divisions. Most upper- and upper-middle-class people live in the urban areas concentrated in the Meseta Central, close to the capital. These areas are characterized by a higher number of motorized vehicles and a wider distribution of telephones and television sets.

Cities, towns, and most villages are divided into *barrios*, or neighborhoods. Most ticos identify strongly with their own barrio, although the upper-class citizens might identify themselves as Costa Ricans or even as citizens of the world. The lower-income barrios tend to be more closely knit, since residents often rely on each other for mutual aid. With the deterioration of the economy in the 1980s and early 1990s, though, even those traditionally close barrio relationships have faded. People move around more, always seeking to improve their conditions, and crime rates, especially for robbery, have increased. In some wealthier urban neighborhoods, a watchman might be employed to protect the area.

Cities, towns, and villages in the highlands are usually laid out in a grid pattern, arranged around a plaza with a fountain, colorful plants, benches, and a bandstand. The main government buildings and businesses are situated as closely as possible to the center of town. The larger towns have schools, restaurants, hotels, a bus station, a hospital, and a large covered marketplace.

Rural settlements, in contrast, are still characterized to some degree by a lack of streets, blocks, and sidewalks, and the absence of a municipal water supply, electricity, and other urban services. They have a central plaza that is usually no more than a grassy square used for soccer. There will usually be a school nearby; a *pulpería* (pool-pay-REE-ah), or general store; and a small church where a visiting priest will conduct Mass once or twice a month. In some places the same building serves as the school and church.

Urban centers in Costa Rica, such as the capital of San José, are characterized by organized streets and public services, such as water, electricity, and schools.

HOUSING

The wealthier urban residents usually live in one- or two-story houses, with a low front porch and a well-kept lawn in front, enclosed by a fence and gate, and a patio courtyard in the middle of or behind the house. Most houses have iron grilles over their windows, and the owners may keep one or two guard dogs.

In contrast, poor urban residents often live in unpainted shacks or in deteriorated buildings that have been divided into crowded apartments. These makeshift dwellings make up the slums of Costa Rican cities. The floors of the shanties may consist of packed dirt, wooden planks, or broken tiles. Lower-class urban workers fashion homes for themselves from these poor materials and keep them as neat and clean as conditions permit.

Rural and poor areas in Costa Rica still lack access to many of the most common amenities of modern life, such as clean drinking water and electricity.

HEALTH AND LONGEVITY

Costa Rica has one of the highest standards of health care in Central America. The Ministry of Health emphasizes preventive measures to ensure a healthy population, including programs that provide potable water, prevent malnutrition, and immunize against diseases. Among its successes is the government-run Program for Rural Health, which extends a network of health units throughout the country to the most rural areas and works to prevent illness through preschool education and nutrition centers. In 2013 there were 1.1 doctors for every 1,000 residents and 1.2 hospital beds for every 1,000 residents. Although the health-care system is still not easily accessible in the more isolated areas of the country, life expectancy has risen to 76 years for males and 81 years for females. The infant mortality rate—8.3 deaths per 1,000 births in 2016—is also far below that of most Latin American countries.

Tropical diseases are common in Latin America, including Costa Rica. Vector-borne diseases such as Zika and malaria are transmitted by mosquitos, while Chagas is communicated via kissing bugs, a vector for the parasite *Trypanosoma cruzi*. In 2016, the Centers for Disease Control encouraged residents and tourists in Costa Rica to take precautions against Zika, which can cause microcephaly, a birth defect for children born to

Costa Rica's robust wilderness is home to many carriers of tropical diseases, including the kissing bug, which transmits a parasite causing Chagas disease.

women who contract the disease while pregnant. People protect themselves from these diseases by installing screens in their windows and doors to keep bugs out, using insect spray, and making sure there is no standing water around their house.

Costa Rica has been recognized internationally for its declining rate of population growth. In 1960, the country showed a 4 percent annual rate of natural increase. By 1973, the rate of natural increase had dropped to 2.5 percent, one of the sharpest declines in the world. During this period, the number of surviving children born to the average Costa Rican woman was reduced from 7.3 to 4.1 children. By 2006, the rate of natural increase had dropped to just 1.45 percent, and in 2016 it was 1.2 percent.

Alcohol use and abuse by young Costa Ricans is a growing problem. Drunkenness is discouraged, but the consumption of alcohol accounts for a large portion of leisure activities. The culture of machismo exacerbates the problem, since refusal to drink may be viewed as effeminate. Some observers of Costa Rican society also feel that the rapid social, economic, and cultural changes of the past few decades have contributed to disorientation and instability within the culture, provoking a rise in both alcohol and drug abuse.

MAJOR EVENTS

Costa Ricans consider family to be the cornerstone of society. Their closest relationships are usually derived from within the family, and they spend much of their leisure time with their relatives. With the declining birth rate, large families are now less common. Couples often decide to have fewer children because they do not want to spread their resources too thinly. It is also not unusual for children to live with their parents until they marry.

DAILY ROUTINES

The daily routine and diet of ticos depends on their occupation and social class. The average urban Costa Rican men and children rise around five or six o'clock, and take a cold shower or bath. After dressing neatly, they present themselves at the breakfast table, where the women have prepared a simple meal of coffee, rice, and beans. They leave for work or school early and may return home for the midday meal. These days, fewer ticos take the time to enjoy a midday siesta, or nap, before returning to work or school.

On the way home, the husband may stop by a cantina, or bar, for an hour or so before returning home for dinner. He plays with his children before they have a light supper. After dinner, he may either stay at home watching television or listening to the radio, or return to the cantina while his wife finishes the housework or sews. The older children either stay at home or go out with their friends. Most do not spend much time studying. On normal evenings, family members go to bed by 10:00 or 11:00 p.m.

Costa Ricans love and cherish children. Women generally celebrate their first pregnancy and welcome one or two more babies. Most births occur in a hospital or health center, which has contributed to the decline in infant and maternal mortality rates. Parents still choose godparents (*padrinos*) for the baby, although the role of the godparent is no longer as important as in the past. Traditionally, godparents were expected to assume responsibility for the religious instruction of the godchild. In this manner, they also contribute to the child's upbringing and education.

Boys generally experience more freedom and less discipline than girls, reflecting the machismo of the larger society. The mother usually acts as the chief disciplinarian in the family. Girls are taught to manage the household, while boys are taught to do the outdoor tasks, such as chopping wood and herding cattle. Many lower-class children in urban areas begin work at an early age to help support the family.

Costa Rica boasts a literacy rate of 98 percent, the highest in Central America. This is the result of the long-standing priority that the Costa Rican government has placed on its education system. In the 1869 constitution, Costa Rica became one of the first countries in the world to make education compulsory and free. This progressive program was paid for largely through coffee revenues. Since the 1970s, Costa Rica has devoted part of the national budget to education.

Schooling is compulsory through the ninth grade for children between the ages of six and fifteen. This includes six years of primary education and three years of a basic secondary education. Students who pass their examinations after three years can choose to take two years of specialized course work. They may study academic subjects, agriculture, or various technical subjects. There are six universities in Costa Rica and several regional colleges. Many students from upper-middle- and upper-class families go abroad to study at a university in the United States or Europe.

Although girls are still more restricted than boys in their social activities, dating couples are common these days. Couples typically enjoy an engagement of two or three months before getting married. The night before the wedding, the bride's family hosts a party for relatives and friends. Everyone brings a gift for the bridal couple, and they enjoy several hours of drinking and dancing. The wedding usually takes place in a church, with

Free education for all is a point of national pride in Costa Rica.

a traditional Roman Catholic ceremony, after which the bride's family hosts another reception for the wedding party.

Costa Rican culture increasingly emphasizes the advantages of youth, but people still feel an obligation to care for their aging parents, either by sending them money or taking them into their homes. Once a person dies, the legal requirement is that the funeral must be held within twenty-four hours, as the body of the deceased is not embalmed. Information about the death and details of the funeral are placed in the newspaper or broadcast on television. As many family members as possible gather for the funeral service. It usually takes place in a church, after which the mourners accompany the casket to the cemetery. Many Costa Ricans prefer to be interred in mausoleums rather than buried in the ground.

Because Costa Ricans have very close family ties and there is no embalming process, mourners are afforded little time to deal with the death of loved ones. Family members are tasked with the immediate obligation of dressing the deceased, and sometimes putting makeup on them to improve their appearance at the funeral.

The law requires that funerals in Costa Rica take place within twenty-four hours of death.

INTERNET LINKS

http://costarica-information.com/about-costa-rica/people-culture-religion/culture/traditions
This website gives a detailed account of Costa Rica's traditions.

http://gocentralamerica.about.com/od/costaricaweddings/p/CRWeddingTrad.htm
This website gives information on weddings in Costa Rica.

RELIGION

Religion plays an important cultural role in Costa Rica, though it is practiced casually by most.

THOUGH FREEDOM OF RELIGION IS guaranteed to all denominations and religions, Roman Catholicism is the official religion of Costa Rica, according to the 1949 constitution. Many Costa Ricans are casual about their religious practices, and only 45 percent of Catholics in Costa Rica consider themselves practicing. For the most part, ticos see Catholicism as an opportunity to observe important milestones in their lives, such as baptism, first communion, weddings, and funerals.

8

Because Catholicism is taught in primary and secondary schools, its influence remains strong as Costa Rica becomes increasingly secular.

NATIONAL RELIGION

Indications of a religious background pepper the speech of Costa Ricans. Many people say, "Go with God," to someone leaving on a trip or even running a simple errand. In response to any inquiry about their health, many will reply, "Fine, thanks to God." When expressing hopes about future events, they will conclude their comments with "Si Dios quiere," analogous to the English phrase "God willing."

They also often thank someone for a gift or favor by saying, "May God repay you." Despite such common expressions of faith in God, most

Although the people have a relatively weak religious culture, many believe in the powers of Roman Catholicism's many saints. Most pray to one or more saints for intervention or protection in their daily lives. The saint most commonly appealed to is probably the Virgin Mary, the mother of Jesus. Other popular saints include those who are associated with a particular situation, such as traveling or the protection of infants and children. Believers express their devotion to the saints by placing small statues or pictures of the saints in their homes or cars.

Costa Rica has its own patron saint, the Virgin of Los Angeles, or La Negrita. According to legend, in 1635 an indigenous woman found an idol of the saint in the place where the Basilica of Cartago is today. Though she attempted to take the figure home with her multiple times, it always vanished and reappeared where she had found it. In 2014, the Vatican agreed to keep a replica of the Virgin of Los Angeles after former president Laura Chinchilla met with the pope.

Costa Ricans are not very fervent believers. Few people, besides elderly people and young girls, go to confession or take communion more often than once a year.

SPIRITUAL REVIVAL

During the last few decades, the Roman Catholic Church in Costa Rica has been undergoing a movement of spiritual revival. Several thousand ticos have become followers of an evangelical, charismatic movement. The church terms this movement Spiritual Renovation, although some people refer to it as Catholic Pentecostalism. Believers may speak in tongues, engage in prophesy, and be physically overcome with spiritual utterances and movements.

The move toward spiritual revival within the Catholic Church can be seen in part as a competitive response to the rising influence of evangelical Protestantism in Costa Rica and all of Latin America. Fundamentally, the movement reflects an effort by the Church to engage ticos more deeply in their faith.

A spiritual revival has created a new enthusiasm for religion across Costa Rica.

In conjunction with the budding revival of the 1970s, some members of the Church leadership rejected both communist and liberal economic development philosophies and began to advocate liberation theology, which emphasizes the need for social and political reforms within society.

PLACES OF WORSHIP

Places of worship vary in their degrees of opulence or simplicity, from the beautiful Basílica of Our Lady of the Angels (Basílica de Nuestra Señora de los Angeles) in Cartago to the simple thatch-roofed evangelical church in a small village. Universal features of Roman Catholic churches, regardless of their size or luxury, include statues and pictures of saints.

Protestant churches also vary in style. Many of the evangelical churches are newer and simpler in style, reflecting not only the lower socioeconomic status of some of the congregations but also their belief that the church is "made up of people instead of walls."

OTHER RELIGIONS

Although Catholicism enjoys its status as Costa Rica's official religion, the constitution grants freedom to other religions as well. Protestants form the second-largest religious group, from mainstream Methodists and Baptists to Pentecostal denominations such as the Assemblies of God.

Other religions include Jehovah's Witnesses, a few Chinese folk religions, Judaism, and some indigenous group religions. One-third of the Costa Rican Chinese population is affiliated with the Catholic Church. There are also some remnants of African religious traditions on the Caribbean coast.

TRADITIONAL BELIEFS AND FOLKLORE

Today's ticos are not as superstitious as their parents and grandparents were. Nevertheless, many still believe that certain people have the power to do good or evil. They may attribute the source of such power to magical, psychic, or supernatural forces.

Some Costa Ricans regularly exercise preventive measures to counteract the possible effects of evil. They may burn incense on Tuesdays and Fridays, when *brujos* (BROO-hos), or witches and sorcerers, are believed to be most active. As water is believed to have supernatural cleansing powers, some people keep a glass of water in the bedroom at night to ward off burglars and illness. While they may not be as superstitious as their forebears, most ticos still maintain a strong belief in the forces of good or bad luck.

FOLK MEDICINE

Costa Ricans tend to mix modern medicine with alternative methods of treatment, such as homeopathic medicine or appeals to saints, spirits, and God. Whatever method of healing they seek, the people believe that faith is the most important ingredient. If their prayers, medicines, or herbs fail to produce hoped-for results, they generally blame themselves for a lack of faith.

Folk medicine is more widely practiced in the rural areas, where people have severely limited access to modern health care. Many rural residents attribute serious illnesses and death to the will of God, if not to an evil spell of a brujo. If they believe that bad magic has been used against them or their belongings, they may try to purify the affected objects with disinfectants and lemon juice to counteract the spell.

Many ticos also believe that food and other substances have hot and cold properties. "Hot" foods include coffee, liquor, and pork. It is believed that these can irritate the digestive system. One can "refresh" the liver (believed to be the organ most likely to be affected by "hot" foods) by ingesting "cool" fruits such as pineapple or watermelon. "Cold" foods, on the other hand, include sardines and to some degree all fish or seafood. These foods are likely to cause stomachaches, for which the remedy is a "hot" substance such as chamomile tea.

Many ticos put their faith in folk medicine, which relies on herbs and rituals for healing.

INTERNET LINKS

https://www.britannica.com/place/Basilica-of-Our-Lady-of-the-Angels
This website gives information on Costa Rica's famous basilica.

http://www.catholic.org
Catholic.org is home to information on Catholism, as well as the practices of Catholics in specific locations.

LANGUAGE

The national language of Costa Rica is Spanish, but many languages are represented in this country.

9

LIKE IN MANY OF THE SOUTH AND Central American countries once dominated by Spain, Spanish is the official language of Costa Rica. However, a large immigrant population means that a variety of languages are spoken, including English and indigenous languages.

EVOLUTION OF A LANGUAGE

There is little regional variation in the spoken Spanish of Costa Rica. Like most Latin Americans, Costa Ricans speak a non-Castilian Spanish—that is, they do not speak the exact Spanish that originated in the Castile region of Spain. The Spanish that Costa Ricans speak has evolved from the language of the first Spanish settlers. Costa Ricans tend to speak Spanish a little more slowly and clearly than many Latin Americans.

Spanish uses a Roman alphabet that has only a few differences from the English alphabet. Traditionally, *ch*, *ll*, and *rr* were considered to be single, separate letters in Spanish. The letter *ñ* is also a separate letter. However, all this is now changing, and not all Spanish dictionaries treat those letters as separate letters.

Costa Ricans like to embellish their language with elaborate phrases and flowery expressions, especially in writing. They lace their speech with archaic words that make their spoken and written expressions formal and courteous. For example, even in everyday speech, Costa Ricans commonly use the archaic familiar form of you—*vos* (BOHS)—instead of *tú* (TOO), which is more commonly used in the rest of Latin America today.

Formal speech is typical of the Costa Rican desire to smooth out the rough edges of social interaction. Flattery and elaborate language are often used, even in a business context. Expressions of courtesy contribute to Costa Rica's image as a warm and friendly society. At the same time, the formality helps to create certain barriers against unwanted intimacy.

TICOS

Why do Costa Ricans call themselves ticos? Most people say that the nickname refers to the colonial saying "We are all *hermaniticos*" (air-mah-nee-TEE-cohs), meaning "little brothers." The substitution of the word *hermanos* (air-MAH-nohs), or "brothers," with the diminutive *hermaniticos* shows the Costa Ricans' historical fondness for diminutizing their words with the suffix -tico.

Throughout Latin America, people often diminutize their words by adding the suffix -ito (EE-to) or -tito (TEE-toh). For instance, instead of simply saying *momento* (moh-MAIN-toh), which means "a moment," they will say *momentito* (moh-main-TEE-toh). People use diminutives to soften their speech, making it more affectionate or sympathetic, or to create familiarity.

Costa Ricans especially like to use the diminutive -ico or -tico, instead of the more common forms -ito and -tito. For example, where most Latin Americans will say *momentito*, Costa Ricans say *momentico* (moh-main-TEE-coh). The ending also acts as a superdiminutive. While many Latin Americans might diminutize the word *chico* (CHEE-koh), or small, to *chiquito* (chee-KEE-toh) to signify tiny, Costa Ricans often diminutize the word even further by saying *chiquitico* (chee-kee-TEE-koh).

The suffix -tico has become an intrinsic part of the way Costa Ricans define themselves. Not only have they adopted it as a nickname, but its very uniqueness is exemplary of the "Costa Rican idiosyncrasy," as they like to say. To describe something that is typical of their culture, they will say that it is *muy tico* (MOOEE TEE-koh), or very tico.

CULTURAL NORMS

Costa Ricans try hard not to embarrass another person or to imply criticism, especially in public. For instance, they are careful not to ask direct questions

Costa Ricans learn to take pride in their idiosyncrasies at an early age.

Although Spanish is the official language, other languages are also spoken throughout the country. Indigenous languages are isolated within the native communities. The largest language group is Bribri, spoken by the people of the Talamanca region. A few indigenous words have been incorporated into Costa Rican Spanish, mostly in place-names.

In an attempt to preserve their language and cultural roots, the Chinese immigrants to Costa Rica set up a Chinese school in Puerto Limón in the 1950s, where language, writing, calligraphy, and history were taught to their children. The school closed down some years later, however, because of the dwindling number of students.

English is also widely spoken. A creole form of English is the most common language on the Caribbean coast of the country. Because of the influx of American immigrants and English-speaking tourists, many Costa Ricans throughout the country speak English as a second language.

that may put the other person in a difficult situation. In a work situation, instead of asking, "Have you finished it yet?" a supervisor may say matter-of-factly, "You haven't finished it yet, no?"

Ticos love to gossip, tease each other, and tell jokes, although they are careful to avoid offending someone directly. Expressions of courtesy are very important, particularly in the context of greetings and farewells. When greeting an acquaintance, whether in a business or social context, a person always asks about the health of the other person and his or her family before discussing anything else. Social acquaintances will extend an invitation to visit when saying good-bye, even though they do not expect the other party to accept the invitation.

Before the contentious World Cup semifinal match between Costa Rica and Brazil in 2009, the Costa Rican coach, Rónald González, greeted the opposing coach warmly.

When visiting someone, especially in rural areas, an individual calls out at the door, "*Upe!*" (OO-pay), instead of knocking—there is no real translation of "upe!" When entering someone's house, a visitor says, "*Con permiso*" (KOHN pair-MEE-soh), or "With your permission." People also say "con permiso" when passing someone in a crowded room or on a bus.

In Costa Rican households, the first thing that someone says on seeing another family member in the morning is, "How did you awaken?" The standard response is, "Well, fortunately, and you?" Such courtesies exemplify the Costa Rican desire for quedar bien, or getting along.

COMMON EXPRESSIONS

A peculiarity of Costa Rican Spanish is the ubiquitous use of *tiquismos* (tee-KEES-mohs), that is, expressions that are used uniquely by ticos. Some examples are simply tico slang words and phrases, such as *buena nota* (BWAY-nah NOH-tah), which literally means "good note" but signifies "cool" or "okay" in Costa Rica. Another expression is ¡*pura vida*! (POO-rah VEE-dah), literally "pure life," but used to say "great!" or "terrific!"

Ticos, like other Latin Americans, also like to use a lot of labels intended as endearments, although they might be considered insults in another country or in less friendly contexts. For example, a tico might affectionately call someone *flaco* (FLAH-koh) or *gordo* (GOR-doh), meaning "skinny" and "fat," respectively, regardless of the person's appearance. They will openly refer to someone of Chinese descent as *chino* (CHEE-noh), or someone of Afro-Caribbean descent as *negro* (NAY-groh). Young men often call each other *maje* (MAH-hay), which literally means "dummy," though they use it to mean "buddy" or "pal."

Costa Ricans also commonly call each other, even complete strangers, *mi amor* (mee ah-MOR), "my love," as a friendly form of address. They toss around such endearments readily, contributing to their image as a warm and friendly people. The affection is generally well meaning but superficial.

The common saying "pura vida" literally means "pure life." It symbolizes the Costa Rican mentality of living for enjoyment but also acts as a note of enthusiasm.

Although the word *adios* generally signifies a good-bye of considerable duration, ticos often use it as a casual greeting. For instance, if an individual passes an acquaintance on the street, he or she might call out, "Adios!" before continuing on his or her way.

Nonverbal communication is often just as important as the words themselves. Costa Ricans do not kiss each other in greeting and good-byes the same way as other Latin Americans. Men always shake hands with each other, but women usually greet each other and men with a kiss on the cheek if they are old friends or family, or even if they were meeting for the first time. The kiss is executed by touching cheeks and kissing the air. Otherwise, if they were meeting for the first time, they pat each other on the left arm. Costa Ricans do not expect foreigners to be familiar with their custom of greeting one another with a kiss on the cheek.

FORMS OF ADDRESS

Costa Ricans follow the Spanish custom of forming a double surname by taking the family surname from both parents. For instance, a young woman by the name of Silvia Calderón Guardia has two surnames: Calderón from her father's family and Guardia from her mother's family. Formally, she is known as Señorita Calderón or as Señorita Calderón Guardia. However, the father's name carries more weight. If she marries a man by the name of

Costa Rica's criminal code makes it a crime, punishable by a prison sentence, to offend another person's dignity and honor, whether face to face or through a written or spoken message.

Rafael Hurtado Velez, she takes his patrimonial surname and adds it to hers, becoming Silvia Calderón de Hurtado. Formally, she is now known as Señora de Hurtado.

After the first full mention of men's two surnames, they are subsequently usually called by their father's surname, although some may prefer to use their double surnames. For example, the current president, Luis Guillermo Solís Rivera, is known as Solís, while Juan Rafael Mora Porras (who served as president in the late nineteenth century) is referred to as Mora Porras.

In the Caribbean coastal area, English-speaking ticos use a more casual style of address, calling a person by the first name preceded by Mister or Miss; for example, Silvia Calderón Guardia would be addressed as Miss Silvia.

Titles are very important in Costa Rica, both socially and professionally. People use titles with their names whenever possible. The most common professional titles are lawyer, architect, engineer, or professor. The most illustrious professional title is that of doctor. Everyone, of course, carries the right to bear the social titles *señor* (say-NYOR), *señora* (say-NYO-RAH), or *señorita* (say-nyoh-REE-tah), which respectively signify Mr., Mrs., and Miss.

A more prestigious social title is still affectionately bestowed on certain people of distinction. Its roots reach back to the minor class divisions of the colonial period. Although everyone was poor during the colonial period, members of the gentry class were called by the honorary title of *don*, or sir. Women of this class were called *doña*, or madam. Two examples of men who have been unofficially honored as gentry in the modern democratic republic include the "father of the revolution," Don Pepe Figueres, and another former president, the Nobel laureate Don Óscar Arias.

INTERNET LINKS

http://www.donquijote.org
Don Quijote is a Spanish language website with cultural information about various Spanish-speaking countries.

http://www.omniglot.com/writing/spanish.htm
Omniglot, an online encyclopedia of languages, offers a history of the Spanish language.

ARTS

Costa Rica has entered a new period in the arts, cherishing work by local artists for the first time in centuries.

10

S PANISH INFLUENCE OVER LIFE IN Costa Rica has not been limited to government and language. Europe has consistently provided Costa Rica with inspiration in the arts as well, leading some to believe that pursuing the arts was only for the wealthy or elite. This view has restricted the development of an artistic tradition that is uniquely Costa Rican. Fortunately, this has changed in recent years, and the arts have flourished.

PERFORMING ARTS

As with other forms of artistic expression, the performing arts suffered from a lack of encouragement and active interest until the latter half of the twentieth century, when attitudes began to change, due in part to immigrant playwrights, musicians, and actors from other Latin American countries, and to the participation of young people in arts programs in the schools.

MUSIC

The best example of the dramatic change in appreciation for the arts in Costa Rica is the Costa Rican National Symphony. Before 1970 it

Aquileo J. Echeverría is known as Costa Rica's national poet. In the late 1800s, he gained recognition throughout Central America for his observations in metrical verse about his fellow ticos. His best-known collection of poems, *Concherías*, describes the Costa Rican landscape and people.

The Costa Rican National Symphony has grown in size and accomplishment since the 1970s.

was a small orchestra that performed a few concerts each year and played mostly European classical music from the nineteenth century. In the 1970s, American Peace Corps worker Gerald Brown was hired to conduct the National Symphony. He revitalized it by recruiting many young foreign musicians to teach their skills to children and adolescents. Costa Ricans are now proud of their National Symphony, which travels around the country to perform concerts, often playing the works of Costa Rican composers. The symphony has also toured internationally and has performed at the White House in Washington, DC, and at the United Nations in New York City.

Costa Rican composers include Julio Mata Oreamuno, who composed *Suite Abstracta* (soo-EE-tay ahb-STRAK-tah) and the operetta *Toyupán* (toh-yoo-PAHN); Julio Fonseca Gutiérrez, who composed a symphony, *Fantasía Sinfónica* (fan-tah-SEE-ah seen-FOH-nee-kah), inspired by Costa Rican folk songs; and Andrés Soto, who has collaborated with organizations in the United States and around the world. Soto's composition *Swashbuckler* debuted at Carnegie Hall in New York City in October 2015. Also noteworthy is César Nieto, who wrote a ballet, *La Piedra del Tóxil* (lah pee-AID-rah del TOH-heel).

DANCE

Ticos love to dance. Outside the concert halls, young people enjoy listening to American rock music, but for dancing, they love Latin and Caribbean rhythms. Every town has at least one dance hall or cantina where people dance to *cumbia* (COOM-bya), salsa, merengue, and lambada, and do the Costa Rican swing.

Instrumentation in popular music usually consists of the marimba and guitar. On the Caribbean coast, drums and banjos prevail, beating out the rhythmic *sinkit* (SEEN-keet) and the *cuadrille* (kwah-DREE-yay). The latter is a maypole dance in which the participants each hold the end of a brightly colored ribbon tied to the top of a bare tree trunk or pole. As they dance, they intertwine the ribbons, braiding them down the pole.

Indigenous dances such as the Danza del Sol (DAHN-sah del sohl), or Dance of the Sun, and the Danza de la Luna (DAHN-sah day lah LOO-nah), or Dance of the Moon, have been preserved by the Chorotega. They have also popularized the musical instruments used in these dances, including the *chirimía* (che-ree-MEE-yah), similar to an oboe, and the *quijongo* (kee-HOHN-goh), which is a single-string bow with a gourd resonator.

Traditional dances are a prominent feature in local and national festivals.

The Boruca people still perform the Danza de los Diablitos (DAHN-sah deh los dee-ah-BLEE-tohs), or Dance of the Devils. The music of the Boruca, the *talamanca* (tah-lah-MAHN-kah), has continued to evolve as they have gradually replaced their traditional flutes and drums with guitars and accordions. One such traditional instrument is the *dru mugata* (droo moo-GAH-tah), a small potato-shaped instrument made of beeswax with a mouthpiece and holes, which resonates with a soft, deep sound.

THEATER

So popular is the theater in Costa Rica today that some say the country has more acting companies per capita than any other nation in the world. The dramatic arts received a boost in the early twentieth century when drama was established as part of the school curriculum. The most important source of inspiration, however, was provided by the influence of playwrights and actors from Chile and Argentina who immigrated to Costa Rica around 1900.

San José offers the greatest selection of dramatic arts. From the National Theater to the numerous smaller theaters, ticos can watch comedy, drama, mime, and puppet-theater productions. In the capital city, theatergoers also have opportunities to watch international productions, in addition to local and national performances.

LITERATURE

The most significant ingredient in Costa Rican literature has been *costumbrismo* (cohs-toom-BREES-moh), or local color. Novelists and short-story writers have tried to depict the lives and local settings of campesinos and agricultural workers, often writing in a campesino dialect. One such essayist from the first half of the twentieth century was Joaquín García Monge, a journalist and teacher who published the journal *Repertorio Americano*, or American Repertory. The journal was significant because it attempted to form a common Central American identity through the formation of critical and informative dialogue. García also wrote the first important Costa Rican novel, the landmark *El Moto*, published in 1900. The country's best-known writers today include Ana Istarú, an actress, poet, and playwright; Laureano

A new interest in Costa Rican literature flourished in the early 1900s and has grown over the last one hundred years.

Albán, a recipient of the Magón National Prize for Culture in 2006; and Fernando Contreras Castro, whose works have become important in Costa Rica's national literary heritage.

VISUAL ART

Costa Ricans looked to European painters and sculptors, largely dismissing the works of local talent, until the late 1920s, when Costa Rican painters began to draw on their own culture and landscape for inspiration. Calling themselves the Group of New Sensibility, these painters became more experimental in their styles, breaking out of the rigidity of conventional artistic expression. They succeeded in developing the first uniquely Costa Rican art style, identified by their depiction of local landscapes, villages, cobblestone streets, and adobe houses.

One of the finest artists of the Group of New Sensibility, Francisco Zúñiga, created *Maternidad*, or *Maternity*, a stone image of a child being nursed by its mother. The sculpture now stands outside a maternity clinic in San José. Critics were not kind in their comments about the work when the artist unveiled it, however, and Zúñiga was so offended that he moved to Mexico.

Foremost among the painters in the landscape movement was Teodorico Quirós. He painted the impressionistic *El Portón Rojo* (el por-TOHN ROH-ho), or *The Red Gate*, which hangs today in the Museum of Costa Rican Art. Other members of this group include Manuel de la Cruz, a Picasso-style expressionist; Enrique Echandi, who was influenced by his studies in Germany; and Fausto Pacheco, Margarita Bertheau, and Luisa González de Sáenz. In the 1950s, painters turned to abstract expressionism and scorned the art of the 1920s as an art of *casitas* (cah-SEE-tahs), or "little houses."

The painters of today are finally achieving recognition beyond the borders of Costa Rica, with their more independent renditions of modernist and contemporary art. Isidro Con Wong, from Puntarenas, is a poor farmer turned painter who has won international acclaim for his style of magic realism. He started painting by using his fingers as a brush and the red paste of the achiote seed as his medium. His paintings now hang in several museums in the United States and France.

Farmers added to the overall impact of the oxcart, or *carreta*, by creating a unique "song" for each vehicle. A metal ring placed on the wheel would strike the hubcap as the cart bumped along the road, producing a distinctive chime.

The *Monument to the Costa Rican Farmer*, by Francisco "Paco" Zúñiga, depicts farming life in Costa Rica.

Until his death in 2013, Leonel González painted images of the black residents of Puerto Limón silhouetted against colorful backgrounds. Another contemporary painter, Roberto Lizano, is well known for his irreverent abstract portrayals of the Roman Catholic hierarchy.

FOLK ARTS

In Costa Rica, remnants of pre-Columbian art are relatively scarce in comparison with other areas in Central America where the larger Mayan and Aztec civilizations existed. Costa Ricans value the artifacts that they have found, however, including large statues from the northwestern part of the country and small art works of carved stone and gold. Such rare artifacts are preserved in Costa Rica's National Museum. Indigenous Costa Ricans (most likely the Chorotegas) also produced jade figurines, as well as large granite spheres that continue to mystify archaeologists.

The indigenous population has only recently begun to influence the artistic development of Costa Rica, with pre-Columbian art becoming a source of inspiration during the twentieth century. Pottery crafted in Nicoya, for instance, follows the traditional craft of the Chorotega. The Boruca create carved balsa-wood masks representing supernatural beings. They also make the decorated gourds that are used in the *quijongo* (kee-HOHN-goh).

The best-known example of Costa Rican folk art is the oxcart, or *carreta* (ka-REH-tah), with its colorful designs and brightly painted wheels. The oxcarts were originally used to transport coffee beans over the mountain roads to the Pacific port of Puntarenas for export. The journey typically took ten to fifteen days. During the rainy season, the roads became muddy bogs, so the Costa Ricans devised a solid wheel without spokes that could cut through the mud without becoming stuck. The solid faces of the wheels inspired the wife of a cart maker in San Ramón to design the first decorated

carreta around the beginning of the twentieth century. The idea quickly became a popular custom, and farmers began to take personal pride in their imaginative carts. In the beginning, the carreta designs consisted primarily of geometric patterns and starbursts, set off by black-and-white accents. Later, artists began to add intricate flowers, leaves, vegetables, faces, and even miniature landscapes.

Perhaps the most traditional Costa Rican art form is the oxcart wheel, which gained popularity after a farmer's wife painted his oxcart.

INTERNET LINKS

http://www.madc.cr
Costa Rica's Museum of Contemporary Art and Design (MADC) is home to many works by Costa Rica's best artists.

http://www.unesco.org/culture/ich/en/RL/oxherding-and-oxcart-traditions-in-costa-rica-00103
The United Nations Educational, Scientific, and Cultural Organization shares information on the arts of different nations, including Costa Rica's traditional oxcart painting.

LEISURE

Costa Ricans value their leisure time and enjoy many forms of entertainment, including attending soccer matches.

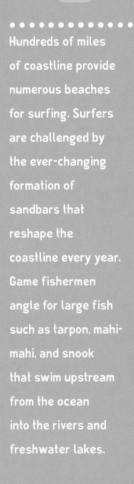

11

TICOS VALUE HARD WORK AND are proud of their reputation as industrious farmers. At the same time, they place a high value on their leisure time. A job is generally perceived as a means to attain a certain level of leisure. While work is necessary to earn a living, leisure is the key to enjoying one's life.

RECREATION

Young men participate in sports more actively than the rest of the population, although this is gradually changing. Older men generally feel that it is inappropriate for them to play soccer, the most popular sport in Costa Rica, although upper-class men might play tennis or golf in private social and recreational clubs. Middle- and upper-class women with leisure time are more active in today's world, taking up some form of exercise as a means of recreation or staying healthy. They swim or play golf or tennis at private clubs.

Soccer, called *fútbol*, is by far the most popular sport in Costa Rica, although it is primarily a spectator sport as it is usually young working-class men who actually participate in the game. Ticos passionately follow the sport at the local, national, and international levels. Every town, small or large, has at least one soccer team. Teams in the smallest leagues arrange their matches by broadcasting challenges to other teams over the radio. The major cities and larger towns all have special arenas

Hundreds of miles of coastline provide numerous beaches for surfing. Surfers are challenged by the ever-changing formation of sandbars that reshape the coastline every year. Game fishermen angle for large fish such as tarpon, mahi-mahi, and snook that swim upstream from the ocean into the rivers and freshwater lakes.

Thanks to the beautiful and diverse landscape, Costa Ricans are able to enjoy a host of outdoor activities, such as swimming, surfing, and hiking.

for soccer games and other sporting events. As a major source of national pride, Costa Rica is the only national team in Central America to have played in the World Cup four times. The team's victory against the United States at the World Cup qualifier in 2016 promised a continuation of their success.

Among the working class, bicycle racing inspires enthusiasm among fans and participants. Team sports such as basketball and volleyball are more popular among upper- and middle-class boys who play for their school teams. Baseball is especially popular in Puerto Limón, where teams are organized and funded by large private businesses.

Men of all social and economic levels enjoy playing pool, be it at the *pulpería* (general store) or in private clubs. Water sports are also popular, especially with tourists. Europeans and North Americans, in particular, now recognize the spectacular advantages of Costa Rica's natural environment for white-water rafting, surfing, windsurfing, and sport fishing. As a result, the tico interest in such aquatic pursuits is growing too.

Boxing and wrestling rank as favorite spectator sports among working-class tico men. Even though ticos are generally peace loving, they enjoy watching professionals fight each other in a controlled setting.

Although cockfights are now illegal, the authorities sometimes allow a cockfight to take place, levying a special tax that goes to charity. People of all social classes enjoy watching horse races, bicycle races, and automobile or motorcycle racing.

COMMUNITY AND COMMUNICATIONS

In addition to sporting activities, ticos enjoy spending their leisure hours socializing, listening to the radio, or watching television. Most of their time is spent with members of their immediate or extended families, although

STORYTELLING

The telling of stories within a group setting is a more traditional leisure-time activity. Television has largely replaced this classic form of social interaction, however, and few young people are familiar with the traditional stories. Some older residents of the Caribbean coastal areas like to gather and exchange stories. Many of the tales originated in West Africa but have been molded by the experiences of blacks in the Caribbean and the Americas.

A favorite character, for example, is Anansi the Spider, a trickster who uses his wits to outsmart larger and stronger animals. In one traditional story, a spell has been cast that says anyone who repeats the number five will vanish. Anansi tricks villagers carrying their goods to the market into saying the number five so he can steal their food, until one day his trick fails and he himself says the number five and disappears forever.

While Anansi is usually represented as a spider, he can also be portrayed as a little bald man who plays a fiddle and performs magic.

increasing numbers of Costa Ricans are joining professional or social clubs and organizations. Leisure time does not necessarily have to be constructive. Many delightful hours are spent simply whiling the time away. Ticos laughingly refer to such idle time as "killing the snake." The expression is derived from a standard excuse given by plantation workers who disappear into the jungle when they are supposed to be working. Whenever the foreman demands to know where they have been, their tongue-in-cheek answer would be that they were out "killing the snake."

In small towns, Sunday is the liveliest day of the week. People dress in their best clothes, and some attend Mass, after which they stroll around town, window-shop, eat ice cream, visit family members, or watch a soccer match. They may travel to a nearby community to visit family members or take a day trip to the beach or mountains. Adolescents socialize with their friends, going dancing or to the movies, or just hanging out.

In larger towns, the streets are usually quietest on Sundays, although the soccer stadium is sure to be packed with zealous fans. Urban residents often leave town on Sundays to visit family members or spend a day relaxing at the beach or at a resort.

DIVERSIONS

Working-class men spend most of their leisure time away from home. After work and on their days off, they may spend hours chatting with friends on street corners or in pulperías and cantinas. They also go to the movies, play pool, and attend sporting events.

The pulpería, or general store, serves as a major social center for a village or neighborhood. Costa Ricans, especially men, gather at the pulpería to watch television, play pool, listen to the jukebox, drink alcohol, and gossip.

The *pulpería*, or general store, is the central meeting place in many small towns. Here neighbors gather to talk and listen to the radio.

Even with television and the internet, the radio remains a popular source of entertainment. It is the most widespread form of media communication. Agricultural workers take a transistor radio with them while they work, women working at home listen to the radio while they do their chores, and office workers leave the radio on at their desks. For many rural residents, the radio is their primary connection to the outside world. Costa Rica has over one hundred radio stations. Most play popular music interspersed with news, advertisements, and soap operas. Others offer classical music or religious, cultural, or educational programs.

Television has become increasingly widespread and popular. However, not everyone enjoys the success TVs have had in the country and around the world. Some ticos blame television for the loss of traditional values and family interaction. Instead of talking together on the front porch or in the kitchen as in previous decades, families often spend their evenings watching television.

Costa Rican TV programs include soccer games, news broadcasts, music videos, game shows, and handicraft and hobby shows such as gardening or sewing. Most television programming, however, consists of old cartoons, situation comedies, movies imported from the United States, or soap operas from Mexico. In recent years, though, there has been an increased access to cable television, especially in the Meseta Central. Channels such as MTV and HBO are now producing shows specifically for the Latin American market.

INTERNET LINKS

http://www.fifa.com/worldcup/teams/team=43901/_index_default. html
FIFA, the international soccer association, provides a profile on Costa Rica's national soccer team.

http://www.visitcostarica.com
Visitcostarica.com lists local attractions and activities for the whole country.

FESTIVALS

The tradition of walking on one's knees on the Our Virgin of Los Angeles Day pilgrimage is more than four hundred years old and brings more than a million Catholics to the Basilica de Los Angeles each year.

12

N THE 1970S, IT WAS CALCULATED that each weekday holiday costs Costa Rica nearly $2 million in lost productivity. Legislators have responded to the concern by moving some holiday observances to the following Sunday or by cutting out others altogether. True to their commitment to leisure time, most Costa Ricans use holidays as an opportunity to go to the beach or mountains with friends and family. Some Costa Ricans complain that their country cannot afford the profusion of public holidays that other countries enjoy, while businesses argue that productivity suffers enough from the holidays they have.

RELIGIOUS HOLIDAYS

Costa Rica's lack of fervent religious devotion is reflected in the people's increasing secularization of religious holidays. Although processions

The Boruca people celebrate the Fiesta de los Diablitos, or Celebration of the Devils, on December 30 each year. The festival has less to do with devils and more to do with the Spanish—the indigenous people reenact the war between the Spanish invaders and the the natives during the sixteenth-century Spanish conquest of the region. In the festival celebration, though, the natives win.

The Christmas celebration is a major event each year in Costa Rica, accompanied by gift giving and the construction of elaborate nativity scenes.

and Masses still take place, most Costa Ricans use religious holidays as an excuse to take a day off from work or school, or simply to have a party with family and friends.

CHRISTMAS Ticos celebrate Christmas with much more glitz and enthusiasm than most Latin Americans. Indeed, Christmas in Costa Rica has all the commercial glitter of the North American holiday season. By early December, ticos crowd the stores and send greeting cards to family, friends, and business associates. Children send their Christmas wish lists to Niño Jesus, the Christ Child, who will send their presents through his messenger, Santa Claus. The *gordo*, or fat Christmas lottery, promises wealth to hopeful ticket buyers. A few days before Christmas, many ticos decorate a cypress tree or a dried coffee branch with bright strips of paper, colored balls, small figurines, and lace.

The only truly authentic Costa Rican tradition is the nativity scene. Families construct elaborate miniature villages around the traditional manger, which remains empty until Christmas Eve. These displays, which may take up a corner of the living room, mix colorful elements of religious and secular symbolism, both past and present.

On Christmas Eve, ticos exchange visits in a whirl of eating, drinking, dancing, and gift giving. At midnight they place the Christ Child in the manger. The family might attend Midnight Mass, after which adults celebrate until dawn. Children may go to bed a bit late on Christmas Eve but rise eagerly in the morning to open their gifts. Tamales, rectangular pieces of cornmeal dough filled with seasoned meat or beans, are traditionally eaten during the Christmas holidays. Stuffed turkey is also served, and it is believed that the Spanish introduced this dish and other exotic foods such as corn, sweet potatoes, and chili peppers to Europe around or soon after the time of Columbus's discovery of the New World.

Easter celebrations often include Stations of the Cross reenactments, which follow Christ's path to the crucifixion.

HOLY WEEK The week preceding Easter has long been one of the most important religious commemorations in Costa Rica. The Roman Catholic Church celebrates the Christian holiday with great ceremony. The observance of Holy Week, however, has become increasingly secularized in the past few decades. More than fifty years ago, businesses closed for the latter half of the week, and a large ceremonial procession would take place in the streets. From Wednesday through Saturday morning, people did not drive their cars and buses did not operate. Today, some businesses close, but more as a vacation than as a religious observance. Fewer people participate in religious processions, and many urban residents leave town for a holiday. In many small towns and villages, however, Holy Week continues to be observed with elaborate processions, rites, and feasts. Some ticos like to travel to such places to experience the more traditional ceremonies.

To bring in the New Year, this man wore a coat made of corn seeds and a rooster on his head in the traditional horse parade.

Caribbean ticos relieve the solemnity associated with Good Friday by playing practical jokes. Calling it Judas Day, they adopted the tradition from the Miskito people of Nicaragua.

On Judas Day, a favorite trick is stealing an item such as a chair, washtub, or plant off someone's porch, taking it to the center of town, and leaving it under an effigy of Judas. Victims of jokes must retrieve their property themselves, while the townspeople jeer and laugh at them. Victims who are too embarrassed to go themselves might pay children to retrieve the items for them.

SECULAR HOLIDAYS

Ticos enjoy any excuse to gather together and indulge in music, food, and alcohol. Most of Costa Rica's public holidays offer an excellent opportunity to indulge the social spirits of its people. In addition to national holidays, many towns celebrate local holidays. For instance, Puerto Limón celebrates a nationally recognized Columbus Day, in a spirit akin to a carnival, as El Día de la Raza (el dee-a day la RAH-sah), the Day of the Race, celebrating not only the human race but also the heritage of Spanish America.

NEW YEARS The most festive part of the New Year's holiday is, of course, New Year's Eve, when ticos gather to drink and dance the night away. It is one of the most boisterously celebrated holidays of the year, serving as the climax of the weeklong festivities from Christmas to the New Year. On New Year's Day, Catholics attend Mass, after which a costume parade takes place and people break open Santa Claus piñatas, which are colorful, hollow papier-mâché containers filled with candy and small gifts. Horse shows and nonviolent bullfights are held as well.

MAJOR HOLIDAYS AND FESTIVALS

January 1	*New Year's Day*
March 19	*Saint Joseph's Day (patron saint of San José)*
March or April	*Holy Week (Thursday and Friday before Easter itself)*
April 11	*Juan Santamaría's Day (commemorating the national hero who fell fighting William Walker in 1865)*
May 1	*Labor Day*
June 15	*Corpus Cristi (religious event)*
June 29	*Saints Peter and Paul's Day*
July 25	*Guanacaste Day (annexation of Guanacaste province)*
August 2	*Our Lady of the Angels Day (patron saint of Costa Rica)*
August 15	*Mother's Day/Catholic Feast of the Assumption*
September 15	*Independence Day*
October 12	*Columbus Day*
November 2	*Day of the Dead*
December 1	*Abolition of the Armed Forces*
December 8	*Immaculate Conception/Holy Communion Day*
December 25	*Christmas Day*
December 28–31	*San José celebrations*

MAYPOLE On the Caribbean coast, English-speaking Costa Ricans celebrate the spring festival known as the maypole. The Miskito of Nicaragua brought the maypole, or *palo de mayo* (PAH-loh day MAH-yoh) with them when they migrated to the Caribbean coast of Costa Rica in the 1940s and 1950s. The festival has roots in old Celtic celebrations in Europe. Now the tradition has spread throughout several African American populations along the Caribbean coast of Central America, from Belize to Panama. The maypole is celebrated not only in May, but also often in June, just for the sheer enjoyment of it.

A tree is decorated with lots of gifts, candies, sweets, and a bottle of liquor. Everyone dances around the tree, after which boys start climbing the

Though more of a Nicaraguan tradition, maypole dances are still a customary part of May Day celebrations in Costa Rica.

tree and taking down the presents and sweets. The revelers eat and drink, with the adults imbibing lots of *chicha* (CHEE-cha), or sugarcane liquor.

Sometimes people follow tradition and decorate a tall, slender post instead. They attach ribbons to the top, and celebrants each take the end of a ribbon. Then they dance around the pole in a special way, braiding the ribbons as they go.

Another feature of the festival is the climbing of a tall pole covered in a greasy substance to obtain prize money at the top. Observers laugh and cheer while the contestants struggle to climb the pole. After someone finally collects the prize, the singing and dancing continue.

DAY OF THE DEAD Celebrated on November 2, the Day of the Dead is the traditional Latin American festival for the dead. Every year, on the Day of the Dead, Costa Ricans celebrate with candy skulls and bone-shaped breads. They carry flowers to cemeteries and mausoleums and decorate the graves of their departed family members. The deceased are so faithfully remembered that they retain an almost palpable presence in Costa Rican society.

CELEBRATING WITH FAMILY AND FRIENDS

Individual communities celebrate *fiestas cívicas* (fee-AIS-tahs SEE-vee-kahs) and *fiestas patronales* (fee-AIS-tahs pah-troh-NAHL-ays), civic festivals and patron saints' festivals. The secular civic festival inspires a great community spirit every year in the smaller towns and villages. The patron saints' festivals are religious in nature, but they feature many of the same activities as the secular celebrations.

In addition to the annual civic festival, towns and villages also hold *turnos* (TOOR-nohs), or street fairs, to raise money for churches, schools, or other

causes. The turno is an elaborate, noisy affair attended by fun seekers of all ages. The fair fires off at dawn with explosions of rockets and usually continues all weekend. Attractions and events generally include mechanical rides, fireworks, and fund-raising bingo games, lotteries, or raffles. The air pulses with marimba music or perhaps with the spirited notes of a band with a guitar, accordion, and maracas. A neighboring town usually attends with its soccer team to play a fiesta game. The inevitable beauty contest takes place, and a queen is chosen from among the young women whose pictures have been published in the newspapers in the days leading up to the fair.

Sugar skulls are a traditional feature at Day of the Dead celebrations on November 2.

FIESTAS CÍVICAS

The annual civic festival fosters community spirit, especially in the smaller towns and villages. In the weeks prior to the fiesta, organizers visit each household with a truck, collecting contributions of livestock, grain, food, or cash. The town council may donate electric power for the event, and local

Food vendors set up stands at festivals to sell a variety of treats and traditional foods.

businesses often donate money, labor, and materials. The fiesta cívica is a grander version of the turno. Food vendors offer tripe soup, rice cakes, beef stew, and other special dishes. Music fills the air, and people dance, play bingo, or go on carnival rides. Bullbaiting, or *corridas* (koh-REE-dahs), is a popular event, especially in the weeklong fiestas cívicas in San José.

Unlike traditional Spanish bullfights, Costa Rican bullbaiting is nonviolent in the sense that the bulls are not killed. A weeklong festival takes place in the small town of Zapote, where young men enter a ring with a small bull.

The men tease the bull by chasing it and trying to avoid getting hurt themselves. They engage in this bullbaiting without the protection of swords or spears, in an attempt to prove their skill and show off their machismo. The events provide as much comic relief as admiration for the daring of the young men. Someone occasionally gets hurt, either from drinking too much alcohol beforehand or from taking too many risks with the bull.

Workers for the Red Cross are often on hand at these events and treat hundreds of wounded men who are gored, trampled, or tossed by the angry bulls.

FIESTAS PATRONALES

The date and style of the patron saints' festivals vary according to the saint and the town. The fiesta usually includes a procession in which participants carry an image of the saint through the streets. Other activities may involve rodeos, dancing, feasting, fireworks, and bullfights.

The most important saint's day for the country as a whole is that of Nuestra Señora de los Angeles, the patron saint of Costa Rica. The history behind her patronage dates back to August 2, 1635, when a tiny black stone image of the Virgin Mary was discovered in Cartago and was removed from the site, only to reappear miraculously. This happened several times. The statuette became known as La Negrita and is believed to bestow miraculous healings.

The Basilica of Our Lady of the Angels in Cartago was built as a shrine in her honor on the site where the statue was discovered. The basilica was destroyed in the 1926 earthquake but was rebuilt in a Byzantine style. Its grandeur and its position as the residence of La Negrita make it the most famous church in Costa Rica. Inside the church is a special chapel dedicated to La Negrita, where pilgrims who have been cured of illnesses leave gifts in her honor. Every year on August 2, people walk from all parts of Costa Rica to visit the cathedral, sometimes crawling on their knees for the final part of their journey.

In Costa Rica, Halloween has become increasingly popular due to commercial influences from the United States.

INTERNET LINKS

https://www.mydestinationcostarica.com/things-to-do/zapote-festival---las-fiestas-de-zapote
This website gives details about the fiesta in Zapote.

http://www.ticotimes.net/2016/07/07/first-songwriter-festival-costa-rica-taking-place-july-6-10
This article discusses the first songwriters' festival held in Costa Rica in 2016.

FOOD

Costa Rica's natural abundance makes the country's traditional foods vibrant and diverse.

13

E ATING AND DRINKING ARE important components of life in Costa Rica. Celebrations and life events are accompanied by traditional meals, and almost every social gathering includes alcohol, usually served with appetizers called *bocas* (BOH-kahs) or *boquitas* (boh-KEE-tahs). Bocas consist of foods such as black beans, chicken stew, or potato chips. It is not particularly spicy but is well seasoned.

In addition to the local cuisine, ticos in the larger towns and cities can eat out at a variety of international restaurants, including Italian, French, Middle Eastern, Spanish, Peruvian, North American, German, Mexican, Korean, Chinese, and Japanese.

COOKING AT HOME

A middle- or upper-class kitchen in the Meseta Central is relatively modern, equipped with an electric stove and refrigerator. Urban kitchens generally have a few cupboards, shelves along the wall, and a small wooden table used for food preparation. A cement or stone sink with a cold-water tap often serves as the washbasin for both laundry and dishes.

Many rural residents still cook with firewood on a cast-iron stove that sits on a wooden or cement platform, with a narrow chimney poking through the roof. These people continue to use wood-burning stoves even when electricity is available, simply because they prefer the taste of food cooked over a wood fire. As recently as 1980, two-thirds of all Costa Rican households cooked with wood fuel instead of electricity.

In rural communities, many meals are still cooked over a wood stove.

In the small towns and villages of the Caribbean region, most residents also cook over wood fires. Modern ovens are relatively scarce, except in restaurants. In many households, the kitchen and the main house are separated. That way, the inhabitants can avoid the smoke and heat of the fires.

The women often build the fire in the open air. When it gets hot enough, they place a heavy cooking pot over the fire and put the food inside, such as bread or dough. Then they heap wood coals or hot coconut husks on top of the lid to provide heat for the top of the food. The cook must have much experience and skill to maintain a constant heat so that the food emerges neither burned nor soggy. If the fire is too hot or if too many burning husks are placed on the lid, the bread will be burned on the outside and uncooked in the middle.

COMMON INGREDIENTS

Costa Rican cuisine, especially in the Meseta Central, relies heavily on starches and red meat, although the ingredients vary according to social class and urban or rural residence. Rice, beans, plantains, and potatoes are the staples. Except for those who live on the Caribbean coast, ticos prefer beef and pork to fish, even though they have plenty of access to fresh seafood.

Costa Rican food is very tasty and judiciously flavored without being spicy hot. Ticos season their food with a mixture of dry spices and sauces that give the food a typical Costa Rican flavor. Some of the most commonly used spices include fresh coriander and mild jalapeño chili peppers.

Costa Rican food combines the indigenous ingredients of the Americas with ingredients and flavorings introduced by the Spanish. A popular dish of Spanish origin is *olla de carne* (OH-yah-day KAR-nay), a classic beef and vegetable stew made with beef, yucca (a tuberous vegetable), potatoes, corn, plantains, squash, and other vegetables.

Gallo pinto (GAH-yoh PEEN-toh), or spotted rooster, is one of the most common Costa Rican dishes and is eaten primarily for breakfast, along with eggs. It consists basically of black beans and white rice, seasoned with onions, sweet peppers, and fresh coriander.

Throughout the country, ceviche (say-VEE-chay), or seviche, is a popular way of eating seafood as an appetizer. Shrimp, shellfish, or perhaps sea bass is marinated in lemon juice, onion, garlic, and coriander, which "cooks" it.

A multitude of fruits are produced in Costa Rica. Fruits grow plentifully in the diverse tropical climates and are widely used in juices, desserts, and side dishes. In addition to melons, pineapples, mangoes, passion fruit, guava, apples, and papaya, ticos also enjoy a host of even more exotic fruits. The fragrant rose apple, for instance, smells like a rose and is best used as a preserve, though it can be eaten fresh in small quantities. The sweet Costa Rican star apple looks like the Malaysian starfruit; when cut in cross-section, it resembles a star. One of the most popular fruits is the *pejibaye* (pay-hee-BAI-yay), a shiny orange fruit with black stripes and yellow flesh. The pejibaye cannot be eaten raw but is a common ingredient in Costa Rican cooking.

El casado is a traditional meal with beans, rice, and plantains.

A TYPICAL MEAL

One of the most famous specialty foods in Costa Rica is *el casado* (el cah-SAH-doh), which means "married man." It got its name in the early days when wives would pack lunch for their husbands, who were generally the only ones in the family who went out to work. Served in many restaurants, this dish consists of a platter of rice and beans accompanied by a variety of side dishes such as cabbage and tomato salad; fried plantains; chicken, fish, or beef; and maybe even a fried egg or fried yucca.

SPECIALTIES

The Costa Rican diet is primarily based on Spanish cuisine but also displays the strong influence of indigenous ingredients, especially corn. The

Like many Latin Americans, ticos love sweet pastries, breads, and cakes. Typical desserts are *pastel de tres leches*, the three-milk cake, and *arroz con leche*, which is a rice pudding.

Cornmeal and meats or cheese wrapped in corn husks, known as tamales, are a favorite at festivals.

pre-Columbian people of Central America centered their lives and cultures on corn, which served as a flour (cornmeal) as well as a vegetable. For instance, they ground dried corn into a fine meal to make tortillas, very thin pancakes, usually topped with meat or cheese.

The Chorotega of Costa Rica also cook tamales, one of the most important festival foods for Costa Ricans. They are rectangular pieces of dough made from beaten corn, lard, and spices. The dough is filled with a variety of ingredients, wrapped in a corn husk or banana leaf, and steamed. The Aztecs introduced tamales throughout Central America, and each country prepares them in its own special way. In Costa Rica, the Chorotega stuff their tamales with tomatoes, pumpkin seeds, sweet peppers, and deer or turkey meat.

People in the highlands subsist largely on the traditional staples of rice, beans, plantains, and corn. Beef is the preferred meat, but chicken and pork are also eaten.

Ticos living along the Caribbean coast eat a lot of rice, potatoes, beans, cabbage, and corn, as well as cucumbers, carrots, tomatoes, beets, and peanuts. These ingredients are mostly imported from the inland regions of Costa Rica. Breadfruit and coconut are locally available. Coconut milk is a popular ingredient for many dishes and beverages. Many agricultural workers gather much of their own food through a combination of hunting, fishing, and farming. Coastal residents enjoy fish much more than the rest of the Costa Rican population, although they eat beef, chicken, and pork as well. Turtle meat and turtle eggs are considered delicacies, although it is illegal to collect turtles or their eggs from the beaches. A typical dish of the Caribbean coastal region is "rundown," a runny, stew-like dish put together with whatever ingredients are available. It always includes coconut milk, some kind of meat or fish, and vegetables. The vegetables are generally the most variable part of the dish but may consist of potatoes, cassava, plantains, or bananas.

BEVERAGES

Costa Ricans drink excellent coffee, since it is one of their main agricultural products. They like to drink it strong, very sweet, and served with hot milk. Campesinos even give coffee to children and babies because they consider it nourishing.

With the profusion of fresh fruits available throughout the year, ticos also drink a variety of juices at any time of the day. The most common fruit juices are mango, papaya, pineapple, watermelon, cantaloupe, passion fruit, and blackberry. Especially in the coastal areas, people like to punch a hole in the top of a coconut and drink the refreshing coconut water. (This is not coconut milk, which is prepared from grated coconut meat.)

Fresh fruits are plentiful in Costa Rica and feature regularly at meals.

Sodas and *batido* (bah-TEE-doh) abound. A batido is fruit juice mixed with milk or water. *Horchata* (or-CHA-tah) is a rather milky beverage made from cornmeal and cinnamon. The preference for such beverages clearly demonstrates Costa Ricans' love of sweets. *Agua dulce* (AHG-uah DOOL-say), or sweet water, is another such drink, containing nothing more than boiled water and brown sugar. The term *refresco* (ray-FRAIS-koh), "refreshment," is a more general term for a beverage.

Alcohol is essential at most Costa Rican social gatherings and festivities. Although ticos like to drink, they do not approve of drunkenness. Two of the cheapest and most widely available liquors are *chicha* (CHEE-cha) and *guaro* (GUA-roh), which are made from sugarcane alcohol, although chicha is sometimes made from fermented corn. Beer and wine are also popular, as are hard liquors such as rum, vodka, and gin. Tico beer is usually light colored, and ticos like to add salt and lime to it.

HOLIDAY MEALS

Perhaps the most popular holiday or festival food is tamales. These are a traditional part of the Costa Rican Christmas feast and are also served at weddings, fiestas, and other special occasions.

Gallo pinto is a simple and common meal in Costa Rica, consisting predominantly of rice and beans.

In Puerto Limón, holiday diners also eat pork cracklings and *mondongo* (mohn-DOHN-goh), a soup made with the tripe (stomach) of a cow. People drink wine, punch, and liquor. They also make their own ginger beer, a favorite nonalcoholic beverage, though they can add wine to it if they want.

For campesinos and many lower-class Costa Ricans, ordinary meals are repetitive and unvarying in their composition. Rice and beans are the primary components of nearly every meal, and gallo pinto practically constitutes the national dish. *Café* (cah-FAY), or coffee, as the morning meal is called, tends to be relatively simple. The midday meal is the heaviest, followed by a light supper in the evening. Ticos snack frequently and drink lots of sweet soda and coffee throughout the day.

In the rural areas, campesinos rise before dawn and eat a simple breakfast of coffee and gallo pinto with a fried egg, or they may have tortillas and sour cream. The women wait on the men during the meal, while nibbling at their own breakfast on the side. The midday meal usually consists of tortillas or white bread, black beans and rice, plantains, and possibly a bit of meat or sausage, with agua dulce to drink. The evening meal is the same.

The urban middle class eats a more varied diet, relying more on processed and convenience foods. They might begin the day with a bowl of packaged cereal or an egg, and freshly made fruit juice, along with white bread and coffee with hot milk. The midday meal usually includes a soup, beefsteak or chicken, plantains, bread or tortillas, a green salad, cooked vegetables, eggs, milk, a fruit dessert, and coffee. The evening meal is very light, consisting of sandwiches or leftovers from lunch.

MARKETPLACES

Costa Ricans purchase their food from three basic types of markets. The traditional marketplace is the open-air market with its many rows of individual stalls. Most towns and villages also have a pulpería, or general store, which sells basic goods and supplies. Larger towns and cities in Costa

Rica have modern supermarkets with well-stocked shelves. Supermarkets provide a more modern but impersonal convenience. Middle- and upper-class women roll wheeled baskets through aisles of refrigerated foods and neatly organized shelves of canned and processed foods.

The traditional marketplace is crowded with close-set stalls offering, for example, hot tortillas and tamales, live chickens or pigs, and colorful cut flowers. Shoppers thread their way through row upon row of fresh fruits and vegetables. Vendors also sell finished products such as leather goods, clothing, handmade baskets, toys, hammocks, and dishes. These markets are found either outdoors or in large enclosed buildings.

The pulpería serves as the corner grocery in city neighborhoods or as the general store in smaller towns and villages. The walls behind the counter are lined with shelves displaying a wide variety of dry goods, processed and canned foods, and staples, including rice, oil, sugar, salt, rum, cleaning supplies, and hardware. Brooms, coils of rope, and woven bags hang from the ceiling. A single shopkeeper usually manages the store, and the goods are generally fixed at a certain price.

As in any culture, food is both a reflection of natural resources—which sorts of foods can be grown in the area—and cultural identity. Because it's a basic necessity, food unifies people and is the focal point of holiday celebrations and family gatherings, as well as an integral part of daily life. It is no different in Costa Rica, where a love of leisure, holidays, and spending time with family provide ample opportunities for feasting.

Other options for food in urban areas are offered by individual specialty stores and produce stands, common in towns and large cities. People often go to the neighborhood bakery or dairy store, or stop by a corner produce stand on their way home from work.

INTERNET LINKS

http://www.cookingchanneltv.com/topics/central-american.html
The Cooking Channel website has many Central American recipes using traditional ingredients.

http://gobackpacking.com/travel-guides/costa-rica/costa-rican-food-typical-traditional-cuisine
This blog features articles discussing typical Costa Rican dishes.

ARROZ CON LECHE (RICE PUDDING)

1 cup uncooked long grain rice
½ cup water
6 cups milk, divided
1 cup canned evaporated milk
½ teaspoon vanilla extract
2 sticks cinnamon, cracked
1 teaspoon fresh nutmeg
1 cup canned sweetened condensed milk
½ cup raisins

Add the uncooked rice, water, 4 cups of milk, evaporated milk, vanilla extract, cinnamon, and nutmeg to a medium saucepan, and bring to a boil over high heat, stirring occasionally.

Simmer over low heat for 5 minutes; then add sweetened condensed milk and simmer for 15 to 20 minutes.

Stir in the remaining 2 cups of milk gradually. Stir until mixture thickens. Add raisins and cook for 10 more minutes.

Serve chilled or at room temperature. This makes 8 servings.

ARROZ GUACHO (STICKY RICE)

3 teaspoons vegetable oil
1 pound lean short pork ribs, cut into 1-inch cubes
1 bunch fresh cilantro, chopped
1 clove garlic, crushed
½ cup red bell pepper, chopped
½ cup onion, chopped
Salt and pepper to taste
1 pound uncooked long grain rice, rinsed and drained

Heat vegetable oil in a saucepan over medium high heat. Add the pork and stir for about 3 minutes to brown, then add water to cover 2 inches above the meat.

Bring to a boil, before lowering the heat. Simmer for 20 to 30 minutes until pork is tender. Stir in cilantro, garlic, red bell pepper, onions, salt, and pepper.

Add uncooked rice and more water to 1 inch above the pork ribs, stirring occasionally until rice is cooked.

This recipe makes 8 servings.

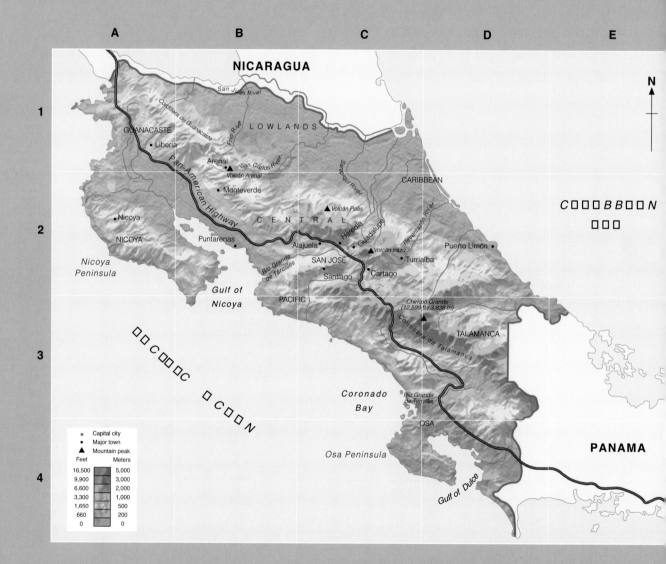

A   **B**   **C**   **D**   **E**

NICARAGUA

N

San Juan River

1

Cordillera de Guanacaste

GUANACASTE

L O W L A N D S

• Liberia

Frío River

Arenal
▲
Volcán Arenal

San Carlos River

CARIBBEAN

• Monteverde

▲ *Volcán Poás*

C □ □ □ B □ □ O □ □
□ □ □

• Nicoya

C E N T R A L

Sarapiquí River

Reventazón River

2

NICOYA

Heredia
•

Puntarenas •

Alajuela •

Guadalupe
•

Puerto Limón •

*Nicoya
Peninsula*

*Rio Grande
de Tárcoles*

SAN JOSÉ •

▲ *Volcán Irazú*

• Turrialba

Santiago •

• Cartago

*Gulf of
Nicoya*

PACIFIC

*Chirripó Grande
(12,599 ft / 3,838 m)*
▲

□ □ C □ □ C
□ □ C □ □ N

Cordillera de Talamanca

TALAMANCA

3

*Coronado
Bay*

*Rio Grande
de Terraba*

PANAMA

OSA

● Capital city
• Major town
▲ Mountain peak

Osa Peninsula

Feet   Meters

16,500   5,000
9,900   3,000
6,600   2,000
3,300   1,000
1,650   500
660   200
0   0

Gulf of Dulce

4

Pan-American Highway

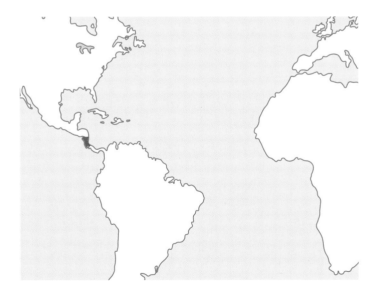

ECONOMIC COSTA RICA

Natural Resources

Hydroelectric Power

Services

Airport

Port

Tourism

Agriculture

Banana

Coffee

Corn

Pineapple

Manufacturing

Electronics

Garment and Textile

Medical Equipment

Sugar

ABOUT THE ECONOMY

OVERVIEW

Costa Rica's economy is increasingly dependent on tourism and industry, while their traditional focus on agricultural exports has diminished. As part of their environmental efforts, the country is also developing technologies to create new green industries and jobs. Its major economic resources include natural attractions, an educated workforce, and fertile land. Costa Rica's strategic location allows easy access to North and South American, European, and Asian markets. Standard of living is relatively high compared with its Central American neighbors, and the country's political stability continues to attract foreign investment.

GROSS DOMESTIC PRODUCT (GDP)

$79 billion (2016 estimate)

GDP GROWTH

4.3 percent (2016 estimate)

LAND USE

Arable land 4.9 percent; permanent crops 6.7 percent; permanent pasture 25.5%; forest 51%; others 11 percent
(2011 estimates)

CURRENCY

Costa Rican colón (CRC)
Notes: 1,000, 2,000, 5,000, 10,000, 20,000, 50,000 colones
Coins: 5, 10, 25, 50, 100, 500 colones
1 USD = 550 CRC (2016)

NATURAL RESOURCES

Hydropower

AGRICULTURAL PRODUCTS

Coffee, pineapples, bananas, sugar, corn, rice, beans, potatoes, beef, timber

MAJOR EXPORTS

Coffee, bananas, sugar, pineapples, textiles, electronic components, medical equipment

MAJOR IMPORTS

Raw materials, consumer goods, capital equipment, petroleum

MAIN TRADE PARTNERS

Malaysia, Netherlands, United States, Mexico, and China (2014)

WORKFORCE

2.3 million (2016 estimate)

UNEMPLOYMENT RATE

9.3 percent (2016 estimate)

INFLATION RATE

3.2 percent (2016 estimate)

EXTERNAL DEBT

$25 billion (2016 estimate)

CULTURAL COSTA RICA

Guaitil Pottery
This small town is a pottery-making center where almost all the families continue the tradition of the indigenous Chorotega group.

Arenal Volcano National Park
Arenal was one of the world's most active volcanoes before it went dormant in 2010. Visitors can experience hot springs and other attractions.

Lankester Botanical Gardens
An impressive collection of orchids and other plants, with trails that sna through desert and forest gardens.

Monteverde Cloud Forest Reserve
One of Costa Rica's most famous nature reserves, which has eight distinct ecological zones and is a sanctuary for a spectacular array of wildlife.

Museo del Oro Precolumbino (Gold Museum)
Contains the largest collection of pre-Columbian gold jewelry in Central America.

Monumento Nacional Guayabo
A major archaeological site believed to be an important religious and cultural center, providing a glimpse of Costa Rica's indigenous past.

Gandoca Manzanillo Wildlife Refuge
This national park is home to manatees, dolphins, and several species of sea turtle that lay their eggs in nests on the beaches during nesting season.

Corcovado National Park
About 124,000 acres (50,000 ha) in size, this park showcases a breathtaking landscape of mountain and cloud forests, mangrove swamps, and beaches. It is also home to a number of Costa Rica's endangered animals.

ABOUT THE CULTURE

OFFICIAL NAME
Republic of Costa Rica

FLAG DESCRIPTION
Five horizontal bands of blue (*top*), white, red (double width), white, and blue, with the coat of arms in a white elliptical disk on the hoist side of the red band; above the coat of arms a light blue ribbon contains the words AMERICA CENTRAL, and just below it near the top of the coat of arms is a white ribbon with the words REPUBLICA COSTA RICA.

TOTAL AREA
19,730 square miles (51,100 sq km)

CAPITAL
San José

ETHNIC GROUPS
White (including mestizo) 90.3 percent; indigenous Amerindian 2.4 percent; black 1.1 percent; unspecified 5 percent; other 1 percent (2011 estimates)

RELIGIOUS GROUPS
Roman Catholic 76.3 percent; evangelical 13.7 percent; Jehovah's Witness 1.3 percent; other Protestant 0.7 percent; other 4.8 percent; none 3.2 percent (2011 estimates)

POPULATION
4.8 million

BIRTH RATE
15.7 births per 1,000 Costa Ricans (2016 estimate)

DEATH RATE
4.6 deaths per 1,000 Costa Ricans (2016 estimate)

MAIN LANGUAGES
Spanish (official), English

LITERACY
People aged fifteen and above who can both read and write: 97.8 percent (2016 estimate)

LEADERS IN POLITICS
José María Figueres Ferrer—president (1948—1949, 1953—1958, 1970—1974)
Óscar Rafael Arias Sánchez—president (1986—1990, 2006—2010)
Rafael Ángel Calderón Fournier—president (1990—1994)
José María Figueres Olsen—president (1994—1998)
Miguel Ángel Rodríguez Echeverría—president (1998—2002)
Abel Pacheco de la Espriella—president (2002—2006)
Laura Chinchilla Miranda—president (2010—2014)
Luis Guillermo Solís Rivera—president (2014—present)

TIMELINE

IN COSTA RICA	IN THE WORLD
13,000 BCE Earliest archaeological record of settlers in Costa Rica.	
1000 BCE Olmec migrants arrive from Mexico.	**753 BCE** Rome is founded.
	116–117 CE The Roman Empire reaches its greatest extent, under Emperor Trajan (98–117).
	600 CE Height of the Mayan civilization.
1502 Christopher Columbus lands in Costa Rica.	**1000** The Chinese perfect gunpowder and begin to use it in warfare.
	1530 Beginning of transatlantic slave trade organized by the Portuguese in Africa.
1561 The Spanish successfully colonize Costa Rica.	**1558–1603** Reign of Elizabeth I of England.
	1620 Pilgrims sail the Mayflower to America.
1737 San José is founded.	**1776** US Declaration of Independence.
	1789–1799 The French Revolution.
1808 Coffee is introduced as a cash crop.	
1821 Central America gains independence from Spain.	
1838 Costa Rica becomes fully independent.	
1859 President Juan Mora Porras ousted from power.	**1861–1865.** The US Civil War.
1870s First banana plantations established.	**1869** The Suez Canal is opened.

IN COSTA RICA	IN THE WORLD
	1914–1918 World War I.
	1939–1945 World War II.
1949 Women and people of African descent are given the right to vote.	**1949** The North Atlantic Treaty Organization (NATO) is formed.
	1991 Breakup of the Soviet Union.
	1997 Hong Kong is returned to China.
	2001 Terrorists crash planes in New York, Washington, DC, and Pennsylvania.
2002 Presidential elections are forced into a second round.	**2003** War in Iraq begins.
2006 Óscar Arias Sánchez wins presidency.	**2008** Barak Obama is elected first African American president of United States.
2009 Costa Rica reestablishes ties with Cuba after forty-eight years.	
2010 Laura Chinchilla is elected the country's first female president.	**2011** Arab Spring begins and is followed by revolutions in Tunisia, Egypt, and Libya.
2012 A 7.6 magnitude earthquake hits the Pacific coast of Costa Rica.	**2012** UN Climate Change Conference extends Kyoto Protocol, to further protect against global warming.
2015 Costa Rica breaks a record for most tourists, with 2.6 million visitors.	**2015** Liquid water is discovered on Mars, suggesting the potential to sustain life on that planet.
2016 The Centers for Disease Control and Prevention announces presence of Zika in Costa Rica and encourages tourists to take precautions. Hurricane Otto makes landfall in Costa Rica.	**2016** Donald Trump is elected president of the United States.

GLOSSARY

absolute poverty
Limited access to basic necessities such as food, water, and shelter.

batido (bah-TEE-doh)
A drink made of fruit blended with water or milk.

bocas (BOH-kahs)
Appetizers.

brujos, brujas (BROO-hos, BROO-has)
Sorcerers; witches.

campesinos
Peasants, small farmers.

choteo (cho-TAY-oh)
Mockery, especially of pretensions or boastfulness.

ecotourism
Visiting natural habitats or attractions with as little impact to the environment as possible.

hidalgo
A member of the gentry class in colonial times.

indígenas (een-DEE-hen-as)
The preferred name for the native population of Costa Rica.

invierno (een-bee-AIR-no)
Winter, also called the rainy season.

machismo
An exaggerated masculine attitude and daring behavior, mostly exhibited by young men.

maje (MAH-hay)
This literally means "dummy" but is often used to mean "buddy" or "pal."

marianismo (mah-ree-ahn-EES-moh)
The concept of a feminine ideal emphasizing self-sacrifice and submission to husband and family.

mestizo
A person of mixed white and indigenous ancestry.

plebeyos (play-BAY-yohs)
"Commoners," or people from the lower class, during colonial times.

pulpería (pool-pay-REE-ah)
A general store that serves as a social gathering place.

quedar bien (kay-DAR bee-EN)
The social art of getting along with others and leaving a good impression.

verano (beh-RAH-noh)
Summer, also called the dry season.

yeoman farmer
An independent farmer who works his or her own land.

FOR FURTHER INFORMATION

BOOKS

Garrigues, Richard. *The Birds of Costa Rica: A Field Guide*. Ithaca, NY: Comstock Publishing Associates, 2014.

Hepworth, Adrian. *Costa Rica: A Journey Through Nature*. Ithaca, NY: Comstock Publishing Associates, 2014.

Koutnik, Jane. *Costa Rica*. Culture Smart: The Essential Guide to Customs & Culture. London, UK: Kuperard, 2012.

Martínez, Óscar. *A History of Violence: Living and Dying in Central America*. Brooklyn, NY: Verso, 2016.

WEBSITES

Arts Culture and Music Costa Rica
http://acamcostarica.com

Essential Costa Rica
http://www.visitcostarica.com

The Tico Times
http://www.ticotimes.net

BIBLIOGRAPHY

Barry, Tom. Costa Rica: *A Country Guide*. Albuquerque, NM: Interhemispheric Resource
 Center, 1991.

Biesanz, Richard, Karen Zubris Biesanz, and Mavis Hiltunen Biesanz. *The Costa Ricans*.
 Prospect Heights, IL: Waveland Press 1982 (updated 1988).

"Costa Rica." The Heritage Foundation. Accessed November 5, 2016.
 http://www.heritage.org/index/country/costarica.

"Costa Rica." Legatum Prosperity Index 2016. Accessed November 15, 2016.
 http://www.prosperity.com/globe/costa-rica.

"Costa Rica Public External Debt." Trading Economics. Accessed Dec. 2, 2016.
 http://www.tradingeconomics.com/costa-rica/external-debt.

Dyer, Zach. "Projected Growth in Tourism Could Be a Jolt for Jobseekers." *Tico Times*, March
 24, 2014. http://www.ticotimes.net/2014/03/24/projected-growth-in-tourism-could-be-
 a-jolt-for-jobseekers.

"Highway from Hell Fueled Costa Rican Volcano." Earth Institute, Columbia University,
 July 21, 2013. http://earth.columbia.edu/articles/view/3109.

Lara, Sylvia, Tom Barry, and Peter Simonson. *Inside Costa Rica: The Essential Guide to Its
 Politics, Economy, Society and Environment*. Albuquerque, NM: Interhemispheric Resource
 Center, 1995.

Lefever, Harry G. *Turtle Bogue: Afro-Caribbean Life and Culture in a Costa Rican Village*.
 Toronto, Ontario: Associated University Presses, 1992.

Lonely Planet. *Costa Rica*. London, UK: Lonely Planet Publications Pty Ltd, 2004.

Nelson, Harold D. *Costa Rica: A Country Study*. Washington, DC: US Government Printing
 Office, 1983.

"Population, Total." The World Bank. Accessed November 20, 2016. http://data.worldbank.
 org/indicator/SP.POP.TOTL?locations=CR.

Spencer, Richard. "Costa Rica Has Only Used Renewable Energy This Year." *Telegraph*,
 March 23, 2015. http://www.telegraph.co.uk/news/worldnews/
 centralamericaandthecaribbean/costarica/11489426/Costa-Rica-has-only-used-
 renewable-energy-this-year.html.

"The World Factbook: COSTA RICA." Central Intelligence Agency. Accessed November 20,
 2016. https://www.cia.gov/library/publications/the-world-factbook/geos/cs.html.

"Your Guide to Costa Rica." Viva Costa Rica. Accessed November 30, 2016.
 http://www.vivacostarica.com.

INDEX

INDEX